Energy Balance

My Guide to Transformation

"In Light & Love" Series - Book 2

Lisa Gornall

Contents

Exercise Contents

Here are all the exercises in the book for easy reference.

Acknowledgments

Thank you to my parents, my sisters, my husband, and my daughters for all your love and support. Life is full of changes and I am glad that you are on the roller coaster with me. I love you!

To my grandmother Dorothy, your light shines on.

Dad, you are the waves.

Foreword

Everything is energy and connects together. At some level, you create your energy and the energy around you. This energy then turns into experiences, life events, and changes. Your life does not just happen to you; you are a creator in your life. You create every experience and change in your life.

Nothing about your life is random. At some level, every detail of your life is planned and shifts with your free will. This means that there are no mistakes in your life. There are no accidents. Miracles are supposed to happen and so they do. They are not random, isolated events. There is no good or bad, everything simply is until you label it one way or the other. Instead of labeling an experience, try enjoying and appreciating it, especially during change.

When you are in the trenches of life-altering changes, it feels as though you have no control and that your life is just happening to you. This is not true. At all times, you are a creator in your life. You may not understand the reasoning behind it for weeks, months, or years, but one day you will look back and know that this was a pivotal and necessary moment in your life. These are the moments that make you want to pull out your hair, but they are also the moments that shape you.

You may wonder why you are having a certain experience or

how everything is supposed to work out when it feels completely out of control. However, at some level, you know this is supposed to be happening in your life because it is actually happening. Even when it feels like things are not going to get better, somehow they do. Instead of trying to figure out why things are happening, ask yourself what you should be doing and do it. Miracles happen and things shift in your life quickly when you let them.

Many different changes are happening in your life in every moment. Some you are excited about, some you do not notice, and others scare you. The question then becomes not why are things happening in your life, rather how are you responding to the events in your life?

Think about previous changes in your life. They may have felt scary, uncertain, and stressful, but they worked out. How did those changes shape your life today for the better? You learned something; there are things you appreciate from that experience, and now you can see why it happened. Knowing that you have survived changes before tells you that you can survive this change in your life now.

Change is Constant

Life is all about change. Multiple changes are around you in every moment of your life. There is no part of your life that is stagnant or on hold. Even if you feel like you are in a waiting place in your life, you are actually in a place of preparation, getting ready for your next experience. Sometimes, this is perceived as the quiet before the storm, but think of it as a space to renew and recharge before the next experience.

Often, the younger you are, the easier change is. Think about a baby and the changes they go through in just a year's time. They go from not being able to do anything but eat, sleep, and go to the bathroom, to being mobile, feeding themselves, and being extremely active. As you continue into childhood and into your late twenties, change seemed fun, easy, and how life should be.

As you get older, you may think you hit a milestone where you think life stays the same. This point in time is where you feel you have accomplished all your plans and goals and life magically freezes. Now change can stop. If only life worked that way! In reality, your life ends when you are done with the changing, growing, and learning of that lifetime. Once you have completed your experience, you would then move onto putting more energy into other lives, not a stagnant one. You are here for the experiences, not a lack of them.

Change does not always seem fun, but it is necessary to help you get to the next level of experiences in your life. Perhaps you feel tired and you would like a break from constant change if that is what you have been experiencing. Sometimes, you will feel you have more to risk and lose if things do not work out, especially if you are in a place of false security. False because you know that life is always shifting and changing, it is not stagnant. You know that things cannot stay exactly the same and yet sometimes you think you would like them to. The changes in your life are essential or they would not be happening. No matter what is happening in your life, you will be okay. You always are.

You may or may not feel you have control over the change in your life. Sometimes, you decide to make a change and sometimes it feels like a change is forced on you. Either way, you are going through a change in your life and the tools in this book will help you through this process.

Every Moment is a Fresh Start

Know that you are a creator, not a helpless victim. In every moment you choose to control, plan, and be out of balance or you choose to surrender, trust, and find your balance. You always choose how to be and how to respond. In every moment you begin anew with a fresh start. Every moment has the potential to be fabulous no matter what is happening in your life; you just have to let it. As you go throughout your day, check in with yourself and see when you are supporting yourself and when you are getting in the way.

During change you may spend more time contemplating the possible end results instead of living your life in this moment. Your focus is often on the past or the hypothetical future, places where you have no power. Your power is now, in this moment. Balance your energy!

In every moment, you choose your response to the events happening in your life. Whether you embrace, fight, or ignore the changes, your response creates your reality and shapes your next moment. Should you control or surrender the situation? Are you afraid to trust the Universe to support you? How balanced do you feel in your life right now? All of these questions you respond to without normally thinking about what you are doing. Now it is time to be aware of what you are doing with your energy and what you are creating, by living consciously.

Your experiences are always helping you in some way, they are not random events. In every moment, you have the opportunity to return to light. Light is how love is shown visually. Love is all there is and you are a being of love. Anything not of love (fear, anger, frustration, impatience, etc.), is an illusion. During intense changes love and light will help you through the process like nothing else.

How to Use this Book

Use this book to find tools that will help you be in a place of balance through all the constant changes in your life. Instead of feeling stuck, overwhelmed, and uncertain, you will learn to feel more balanced, focused, and peaceful. Peace is possible in every moment of your life.

This book builds on the tools and energy work taught in my previous book, "In Light & Love: My Guide to Balance." The exercises in this book are based upon the energy work I do with my clients as they are finding balance and transforming during change.

Throughout this book you will learn how to be aware of your energy and balance it as you are going through your experiences. In every moment, what you do with your energy has an effect on everyone around you. It also influences your perception of how things are going and it creates your reality. You will learn to be aware of what you are creating and learn how to course correct when things are not working out.

Written Spiritually

As you read through this book, know that I use the word "Universe," but you can substitute in whatever word you use to mean God, Love, Light, Source, etc. This book is not meant to be religious, but spiritual, so that you can incorporate it in with your beliefs. Use whatever words support you and practice the exercises to help you become aware of your energy and regain balance.

Miracles are also mentioned throughout the book. I use the word miracle to mean something that happens at the perfect moment, with amazing synchronicity, and it transforms a situation in a way that a person would not have been able to. A miracle is not something that someone can plan or create; it comes from the Universe. Miracles can be simple or big and they happen all the time. If you believe something different with your religion, please feel free to substitute in a different word for miracle when it is used, such as synchronicity or whatever works for you.

Ways to Read this Book

Read through the book first so you can see how everything works together and so you can refer back to specific sections later. Use this book to help you reclaim your balance and focus during change.

There is no right way or wrong way to read this book, just the perfect way for you in that moment. Perhaps you decide to read the book again from start to finish. Sometimes, you may just decide to open the book up to a page and that is what you should read and work on. Other times, you may look at the table of contents and pick a section that applies to what you are working on in your life right now.

As you do the exercises, use them as a guide. Check in with

yourself and see if they will work as they are, or if you should tweak them to your experience in this moment. If you are going back to the exercise only, you may find that sometimes it is helpful to read the section before the exercise for more clarity.

Sometimes, people find it helpful to work through the book at the same time with someone else. This will also help you create support for each other and will help make the changes you are experiencing easier. Always do what works for you and supports you.

Enjoy your journey and if you find yourself having a hard time, use an exercise from this book to help you. Balance is possible in every moment, even during intense changes in your life.

In Light and Love,

Lisa

1 – Change Essentials

The roller coaster lows and highs of life can take a toll on you. Perhaps the lows make you tired, crabby, or irritable. The highs on the other hand have you soaring through the air like a kite, feeling ungrounded, and like all is well when it really may not be. You will notice your body feeling out of balance from these lows and highs. This section will help you find ways to create a safe space anywhere, let go of anything that is holding you back, and teach you how to fill that space with positive energy.

These basics will help you in any moment of your life, but you will find them essential when you are going through life-altering changes. Sometimes, you will do all these exercises back-to-back and sometimes you may only do one or two of them. Always do what works for you.

Finding Balance with White Light

You are a being of love. Visually, this is seen as a White Light that shines through and around you. We are all made of White Light and we are all connected by it as well.

White Light is God, Love, the Universe, Source, or whatever you would like to call it. It is non-denominational, it just simply is. Before we inhabit our bodies, love is all we know. This is our truth and you can return to it in every moment.

White Light is everywhere. You will see the beams of White Light breaking through clouds and trees most often in nature. It is also shown in pictures of religious and spiritual people as a light surrounding them. White Light flows through you at all times. Imagine visually that you are surrounded by it in a huge spotlight or beam of light and it flows gently like a stream through your being. By bringing it through your body, you are remembering that you are love and light, and that all is well.

When you feel out of balance, one thing you can do to get back into balance immediately is to bring White Light through your body. This will instantly balance your being (your body, mind, and spirit), and you will instantly feel calm and peaceful. White Light feels nurturing and supportive because it is. It helps you remember who you really are, a being of love. White Light grounds you and centers you.

White Light Exercise

Use the White Light to return to your natural state of being and create a safe space at any time. You will feel calm and peaceful.

Tips: You can sit or stand; be comfortable. If you lay down, you may fall asleep. Do not cross your arms, legs, or any body parts as this will make it more difficult for the energy to flow freely, especially when you first begin practicing this.

Visualization: Close your eyes. Begin by bringing White Light through your body. Imagine the light beams you see that break through the clouds or shine through the trees. This is your visual to imagine. The White Light is nurturing and supportive.

White Light: Imagine the White Light shining down on you, through you, and around you. The White Light comes in through the top of your crown (top of your head), down your face, your neck, into your shoulders, down your chest and back, into your stomach, into your hips, down into your thighs, to your knees, down your legs, and into your feet. The White Light flows from the center of your feet, down into the Earth. You become one with the light and the light flows into you and into the Earth.

You will feel calm, centered, and at peace. You will be grounded (this is why you bring the light through your feet and into the Earth.) The White Light flows through you like a stream and it looks as if it is a beam of light flowing through you. The White Light surrounds your whole being.

Open your eyes when you are ready.

White Light is not Flowing Easily

The White Light can flow through you at all times like a stream. However, sometimes the light is blocked from flowing through your whole body. For example, you can see the White Light flowing but you do not feel it flowing through your whole body, into your feet, and into the Earth. Instead it gets stuck somewhere or even in multiple places.

White Light is always there, but how much are you letting flow through you? Where is the light getting stuck and why? Sometimes, when you feel tense or if you are in a place of fear, the White Light will stop flowing easily through certain areas of your body. It is almost as if you freeze that part of you to help you with whatever you are experiencing in that moment. However, you will find that if you let the White Light flow through instead of stopping it, you will be in a better place to process whatever is happening around you.

Check in with yourself throughout the day and notice how the White Light is naturally flowing through your body or if it gets stuck somewhere. Just check and see where you are not letting it flow and then let it flow again. You can bring the White Light back through your body and if that does not work, there is letting go to do in that area.

White Light Flows Exercise

White Light always flows through your being, but how are you letting it flow? Check in and see if the White Light is flowing effortlessly or if it is being stopped or blocked somewhere.

White Light: Begin by bringing the White Light through your body and notice where the White Light is not flowing. Know that the White Light is always flowing through your being like a large stream of light. However, how much it flows depends on what you are allowing to flow in to your whole being.

Check in: Is it flowing easily in through the crown of your head or does it feel like something is blocking it? If it is not flowing in through the top of your head, see the next section, "If You Cannot Connect with the White Light." Where is it not flowing in your body easily? Note: It may be one area or several.

Let go: Let go of any tension or blocks in your body which are not letting the White Light flow through easily. You can simply push the block out and imagine the light flowing through again, or you can do a quick letting go session (see the "Letting Go" section in this chapter.) Do whatever works best for you in this moment.

Check in: How is the White Light flowing through your body now? Let go of any more tension or blocks if you find any, and let the light flow through your body again.

White Light: End by bringing the White Light through the crown of your head, into your feet, and into the Earth. It is a steady stream and you feel safe, comfortable, and at peace.

Open your eyes when you are ready.

If You Cannot Connect with the White Light

If you find that you are not able to see the White Light or bring it through your crown (top of your head), do not worry. You are a being of light; you are this light. Something is just happening to keep you from seeing it, but there are things you can do.

Light always conquers darkness. Remember what happens when you are in a dark room? Once you turn on the light, the darkness disappears. The same is true with White Light; it makes the darkness disappear. Love conquers all. White Light is love. The darkness is not real; it is an illusion that easily disappears.

Anything not of love is not real. Darkness, negativity, anger, hatred, etc., are all illusions. They disappear when surrounded with love or light. In our society, you are taught there is always a villain and darkness is always there. If you have not questioned this before, question it now. What happens to the darkness when you send it White Light? Things shift. Illusions disappear when you put White Light on them. When people come together to spread love and light, in that moment, anything that is not of love disappears.

Reconnecting with the White Light Exercise

If you find yourself not able to see or connect with the White Light, do this exercise to help you.

Stand in light: Begin by standing outside under the sun or under a light in your house and let the light flow from your closed eyes through your body. Feel the soft glow of the light on your eyelids and imagine it flowing through your body. Then do it again from the crown of your head, down through your feet, and into the Earth.

Let go: If you feel any tension or darkness in your body that is preventing the White Light from flowing through, then there is letting go to do right away.

You will bring the White Light through your body. Wherever you feel it getting stuck, imagine pushing out whatever is there, even if temporarily, so you can get the White Light to flow through your body.

Then do some letting go if it is still there once you bring the White Light through. ("Letting Go" is in the next section of this chapter.) Always bring the White Light through before you start doing any letting go.

White Light: End by bringing the White Light through the

crown of your head, into your feet, and into the Earth. It is a steady stream and you feel safe, comfortable, and at peace.

Check in: If there is more letting go to do, do it now. Then bring the White Light through your body again.

Open your eyes when you are ready.

Use White Light Daily

White Light is a core element to all the energy work you will be learning and doing. Try doing the "White Light Exercise" at least three times a day. Do it when you wake up and look at the clock, around lunch or your afternoon snack if you do not eat lunch, and when you go to bed and look at the clock. This will help the White Light become a routine that centers and balances your being.

Make sure that this does not just become a routine that you do absentmindedly. You have to do it and really experience it or you will not feel its benefits.

Letting Go

You can visualize White Light and feel the peace it provides you, but sometimes it is time to energetically clean out your being. For example, White Light fills you with love, but if you are already full of negativity, irritation, frustration, or really anything that is not of love, you just keep battling the darkness with White Light. End this energetic battle by cleaning out all this "junk" that is holding onto the darkness.

You will know when you have letting go to do, just pay attention to your clues. Perhaps you feel angry or sad immediately for no known reason. Maybe everything is going well, you feel great, and then you hit a wall out of nowhere. You may feel a nagging pain in your body or tension that is not going away and there is no physical reason for this pain. Maybe you notice it when you are bringing the White Light through and it is not flowing through your body. No matter what the clue is for you, instead of getting stuck there or feeling hopeless, let go of whatever it is. Let go so you can change your focus from the past to this moment. Letting go does not mean that you forget the experience or what you learned, it means you let go of the baggage from that experience.

In life, letting go is essential! You will find that you become a pro at letting go during every major transition and with the small stuff too. From the hiccups with the big change in your life to the driver that cut you off on the road, letting go will help you return to a place of light quickly. You will feel so much better after you let go and you will be in a better place for whatever is happening in your life at that moment.

When to Let Go

When you start to feel overwhelmed, irritable, stuck, trapped, or frustrated, these are some clues that there is letting go to do. Let go of anything that no longer represents who you are, anything that is making you feel stuck or trapped, any fears or beliefs that are no longer serving you, or anything that is frustrating you during this change.

Some things for you to let go of in this change: your expectations of how this change should happen, when this change should be done by, and the outcome from this change. These are big things, but it is important for your ego to step aside so that things can really happen in the best way for everyone. Your ego cannot see that, it only knows to control. Instead, let it go! Then you can trust and flow better through this change.

Become aware of your fears during change because they will try and run the show whether they are logical or not. Fears are experiences from this life or other lives that are appearing now to be healed. Look at your fears objectively and you will see that they often make no sense at this moment in your life. They probably happened at some point in this or another life experience, but they are not happening in this moment, unless you keep recreating that reality. If you do keep recreating it, now is a perfect time to create a new reality without that fear.

Fears make you feel powerless. Instead, regain your power by letting those fears go and healing that part of you. You had an experience that has turned into a fear for a reason. Release it, it is no longer true. You are free the moment you let the fear go and you heal that experience, all at the same time. Try to let go of fears when you become aware of them. Sometimes, they are easy to let go of, and sometimes they take some time.

There are many different ways to let go whether it is through exercise, creating art, journaling, visualizing, etc.; the list goes on! Here is an exercise where you visualize the tension, stress, frustration, etc., leaving your body.

Letting Go Exercise

Letting go helps you release anything that is blocking you so you can be more in the moment. This moment is where you have power; the past is done. Let it go!

White Light: Bring the White Light through the crown of your head, into your feet, and into the Earth. It is a steady stream and you feel safe, comfortable, and at peace.

Letting go: Begin by noticing where there is darkness, tension, or gray smoke in your body. Start with the area that is calling your attention the most. Then, imagine sending that energy up into the sky or the Universe. The Universe is all love. The Universe will turn the energy into love and it will shrink into a speck of pepper before it disappears completely.

You can imagine pulling the energy out like a weed, you can stomp it out, or imagine it flowing out of your body like smoke. Whatever you see and feels right in that moment, do.

White Light: Bring the White Light through again and say your truths, "I am love. I am light. I am safe. I am whole." You can say this as often as you would like. If you resist one of these "I am" statements, check in with yourself and see what letting go you have to do around that statement.

Tips for your body: Sometimes, it helps to wiggle or shake that body part or move your body around if you are having a hard time moving the energy out of your body.

Water is always helpful as well if you are having a hard time moving energy. You may feel a pull to put your feet in water (whether a tub, bowl, pool, lake, stream, or even take a shower).

Showers are a great place to let go. You can do a daily letting go while cleansing the external parts of your body. Bring the White Light through your body as the water is cleansing the outside of your body and imagine any frustration, anger, and stress from the day going down the drain.

Tips for your mind: If you find your mind is holding onto an experience and the details, shift your focus. Instead, be grateful for that experience as you are letting it go. Everything happens for a reason. Why did this happen and what did you learn from experiencing it? For example, "In this experience I learned _____. I am grateful for _____." Thank the Universe for the experiences you have had, especially the ones that seemed harder and really forced you to grow.

Balance yourself: When it feels like the tension, stress, energy, or whatever you were letting go of is less; bring the White Light through your body again. "I am _____."

Check in: Does it feel gone?

If it feels gone, go to next step, "More letting go."

If not, keep going for as long as you can. Remember to stay in balance with your body. If you are feeling that your body has done all it can right now, do more another day. Sometimes, you can let go of "stuff" right away and sometimes it takes more than one letting go session.

More letting go: Is there more letting go to do somewhere else in your body at this time? If you answer yes, release that energy if you can at this moment.

Closing: When you are finished, bring the White Light through your body, into your feet, and into the Earth.

Nurture and support your body the rest of the day, especially if you did a lot of letting go. A nap or early bedtime will help you renew and reset your body after a lot of letting go.

Letting Go Tips

Letting go is like an onion. There are many layers and some may make you cry more than others. Energy moves quickly. Sometimes, you will find the energy is gone quickly and you do not even know what you let go of. Others may take a little bit more time and feel like they have more layers. Remember that anything not of love is an illusion and you can let it go as easily as you let it into your life. Do not try to remember what you let go of, simply let it go.

Only do as much as you can in one day. Stay in balance and pamper yourself, especially after an intense letting go session. Make sure that if you do a lot of letting go in one session that you have time for a nap or rest time after. When you are letting go it may not feel like you are doing a lot, but you may be physically exhausted later.

Everything is connected not only in this life experience, but in others as well. Do not be surprised if you find yourself seeing or knowing of experiences that are from another life. If you are seeing something while you are letting go and you are getting to let go of it, do not question it, just do it. Your mind cannot make this stuff up, trust what you are seeing or feeling and then let it go.

Always make sure you bring the White Light through your body after you finish doing your letting go. This will help balance your being which is necessary after any energy shift you do.

You will find that letting go becomes a daily ritual because you will feel much better after you do it. As you go throughout the day, check in with yourself and literally push anything out of your body that does not belong there. At all times, you are a being of love. This is truth. Anything not of love is not real; let it go.

"I am" Statements

Words literally mean what they say and that is what you create in your life. Now that you are aware of their power, be aware of what you are creating. If you say you "want" something, you will want it and not get it. The same is true with words like need, want, desire, crave, etc. How often are you using these words? Notice what happens the next time you use them, you will find that you keep needing, wanting, desiring, and not actually receiving what you "want."

Use words that help you feel safe, connected, and at peace. What works for you today, may be different tomorrow. "I am" is the most powerful thing you say to the Universe. You can feel the power of these statements flow through your body the moment you think or say them.

"I am" statements that resonate with you will vary depending on what you are experiencing. However, there are some that are always true like: "I am love." "I am light." "I am safe." "I am whole." These statements are always true and you can use them at any time.

Being that "I am" is the most powerful thing you can say, be aware of what you are putting after the quotation marks. Do not add any negatives into your statement. "I am _____," means that you already are whatever you are saying. This statement will resonate with your body.

Using "I am" Statements

Sometimes, you will decide to start off your day with an "I am" that will help you with whatever you are working on as you go through this change. You may connect with, "I am going with the flow," "I am peace," or "I am calm."

Say the "I am" statement while doing the White Light and let it flow through your body. The "I am" is a powerful statement that will create support for you right away. Use it often and with purpose. Keep your statements simple and easy to remember. Then you will be able to use it more often.

Regardless of what you are experiencing, ask yourself what "I am" will help you feel more calm, more balanced, and more supported. Then use that "I am" statement for a few days or until you find another one that is more supportive to you. Write it down and stick it on your computer, in your wallet, on your bathroom mirror, or anywhere that will help you reconnect with it by seeing it often. Your "I am" statement will shift with your experiences.

"I am" Exercise

"I am" is a powerful statement that you can use to help support you regardless of what is happening around you. It helps you tell your mind what to focus on and it supports your being.

White Light: Bring the White Light through the crown of your head, into your feet, and into the Earth. It is a steady stream and you feel safe, comfortable, and at peace.

"I am" statement: Say your "I am" statement(s) and let the energy of the words flow through your body, just like the White Light. Imagine the words flowing from the crown of your head, into your feet, and into the Earth.

Open your eyes when you are ready.

"I am" and Letting Go

"I am" statements are very nurturing and supportive to your body after you have done letting go in that area. These statements support your body and help reprogram that area. An area that was holding onto negativity gets cleared in the letting go session and is now reprogramming into the "I am" statement you are putting there.

While you are letting go, say, "I am love. I am light. I am safe. I am whole." Always say these truths when you are letting go. They will empower you and help you with whatever you are releasing.

Feel free to say them in the order that supports you the most in the moment. If you are using one of these "I am" statements while you are letting go and you feel yourself rejecting it, you have some letting go to do around that "I am" statement. Once you do the letting go, the statement will help you feel more peace and calm.

Then you may use different "I am" statements in different parts of your body. Typically the statement is an opposite statement of what you just released. For example, you may say, "I am free," in your lower stomach where you felt trapped. In your throat you may say, "I am speaking my truth." If you feel abandoned you may connect with, "I am supported." If you feel stuck say, "I am flowing." The shorter the "I am" statement, the easier it is to use.

After letting go each area may have a different "I am" statement or you may just use one for your whole being. Use whatever "I am" statement(s) that will support you in this moment. Make sure it is short and there are no negatives in the statement like, "I am not holding onto this negative energy any longer." Instead you could say, "I am free. I am whole."

Continue to use your letting go "I am" statements for at least three days after you do your letting go or until you find another "I am" that is more supportive to you. Every time you do letting go, see what other "I am" statements will support you with whatever you just let go of and use them with, "I am love. I am light. I am safe. I am whole."

Chapter Reminders

You will notice that White Light, letting go, and "I am" statements are extremely important tools. They help you through change and with all your day-to-day experiences as well. Use them as often as you like. Eventually you will find yourself doing them automatically without even thinking about doing them.

Check in with yourself as you are using your "I am" statement(s) and make sure that what you are saying supports you the most in that moment. You cannot say, "I am" and not resonate with your statement. If you do not believe what you are saying it will not work for you. This often means there is some letting go to do around that statement and then it will work for you.

2 – Understanding Change

You know that change is a part of life. Your life flows from one change to the next, but often, you do not notice the changes unless it is something that shifts your world.

Small and big changes are constantly in your life and they affect you in different ways. You may not pay much attention to small changes, like when one day ends and another begins, or even when the months change. However, you notice the seasons changing. No matter where you live, the climate around you lets you know that it is changing. Whether winter comes by rain and colder weather in San Diego, or snow, blizzards, and ice in New York, you know that winter has arrived. You have learned to adjust your daily life with these changes without even thinking twice about it.

At this moment, you are experiencing changes simultaneously and continuously in your life. Small, big, and life-altering changes are a part of your life and they shape who you are. The small changes usually do not bother anyone. Often they go unnoticed in your fast-paced world. Big changes often make you stop and adjust your course. However, life-altering changes may humble you and turn your world upside down.

Small Changes

Small changes happen all the time all around you. Think about all the small changes you experienced in your routine just today. Maybe you ran out of food you typically eat at breakfast or you did not have a special drink. Perhaps a road was closed on your commute or traffic flowed differently today than it usually does.

You find ways to adjust to these little changes; sometimes they are barely a blip on your radar because they seemed easy. Often you have more control over the outcome of these changes. They have an impact on you for a small amount of time and then you move on to something else. You ran out of your favorite drink, no problem. You may be disappointed, but you will find something else to drink.

All of these little changes show you that life is anything but stagnant and predictable. They also help prepare you for the bigger changes. You know you can survive change; you do it all the time. You just were not paying attention to them to know that they were even happening. Notice that even though you were not aware of the changes or concerned with the outcome, they still happened. Everything worked out.

Pay attention to the small changes happening around you today. Notice how many you experience in one day. You will be surprised to see how many changes happen around you that you did not notice before.

Big Changes

Usually when you are making smaller changes in your life, they are easier to control. These experiences lead you to believe that you can do this in all situations. Then you experience a bigger change and you wonder, what is happening? Why does this seem so hard? Why is it taking so long?

Big changes typically include moving, job changes, relationship changes, or any type of life change that usually has you unsettled for a small amount of time. Big changes are more complicated, involve you more personally, and require your time and attention.

These changes are more intense than small changes. Big changes do not just affect you for one moment or for even one day. They go on long enough to throw you out of balance and send you looking for ways to regain it.

At all times, no matter what is happening around you, remember that you are always supported. You are always love, not loved, there is a difference. The White Light is always there and flowing through your body. Also, you can bring it through your body at anytime, anywhere. Use it as often as you would like. You will find that it is a saving grace and a vital part of your daily routine, especially during change.

Bring the White Light through your body now. Release any tension you are holding in your body. Then bring the White Light through your body again. See how you feel more calm and balanced? Make sure you are using the White Light often because if you are in a better space, you will make better choices.

Sometimes, big changes seem scary and out of control, but when you stop trying to regain control of the situation and the outcome, you will actually feel calmer. The process will also happen easier than you could have ever planned. These big changes prepare you for the biggest changes you will experience, life-altering changes.

Life-Altering Changes

Life-altering changes are exactly that, life-altering. By the end of this change, your life will be different. You will feel different. Not just a big change like buying a new house different, this change will reshape, refocus, and even repurpose you. Life-altering changes do not happen very often, but they are extremely powerful. You know when you are experiencing a life-altering change. This change is more intense than other changes you have experienced, it goes on for a long period of time, and your life will be very different at the end.

This change will help you get back on track with your life purpose. You are here for a reason and if you are not doing what you are here to do, this change will help you do it. This change alters you in such a way that it often changes your thought-out course or plan in life. Life-altering changes help you align with your spiritual plan that you created before you were born into this experience.

As you are going through the process, you probably will not appreciate the changes that you are making or the shifting that is happening in your life. However, when the change is done and some time has passed, you will know that this was a pivotal point in your life. This change will help you become more of who you are, no matter how you resist or fight it. In the end, this change will be critical in helping you become more of who you are supposed to be.

This is a big change that literally brings you to your knees until you completely give up and surrender. You will be okay surrendering because you trust that the Universe supports you in every moment no matter what is happening. Surrendering your expectations, trusting the Universe, and being in balance are vital in life-altering changes. In fact, it is the easiest way to experience them.

Sometimes, life-altering changes seem to go on and on, with no end in sight. Of course, this is not true. All things come to an end. However, in this type of change, you are in turmoil and fluctuation for a larger period of time than you are used to experiencing. How long really depends on how much resistance you are providing, what you are doing and creating, your life plan, and how easily you are able to go with the flow.

Often what you think you would like as the end result, is not usually the end result of this change. Usually you shift so much over a long period of time with this change that there is not just one end result, but many. Finding your balance is often something you are doing throughout the day in this experience.

The highs and lows of this change tell you how to support your body, mind, and spirit in those moments. You will learn to become more aware of your energy and get better at regaining balance when you feel like you are constantly shifting and adjusting.

Even if you feel like you are completely going with the flow, this change may still take quite some time. Remember that there are many pieces to the puzzle and that they will align at the perfect time. Do not worry; there are exercises to help you regain your balance especially when you get frustrated with this life-altering change process!

Balance During Change

In every moment of your life it is possible for you to regain your balance. When you feel like you are being bombarded with things that are out of your control during change, the "Raft Exercise," "Future Visualization Exercise," and "Finding the Light Exercise," will help you get back on track.

Objectively Checking In

Life is a roller coaster. There are highs and lows to help you adjust your course. They offer you a different perspective so you can see more of the whole picture and adjust as things are shifting. The highs help you shift earlier because you are feeling good and willing to make changes faster. The lows often pull you down, making you feel stuck, unsure, and frustrated. However, the lows happen so you can become aware of anything that is keeping you from moving forward so you know what to let go of at that time. The lows also give you some down time to get back in balance.

Life does not just "happen" to you. You are not a spectator along for a ride, although it may feel like you are at times. At some level, you create the changes in your life and your reality. You control how you are responding to the changes in your life.

The "Raft Exercise" is a way for you to objectively look at your situation right now and see how you are responding. How you are responding in this visualization is how you are responding in your life right now to this change. Your response creates the experiences in your life. What are you creating?

Raft Exercise

Check in with yourself objectively to see how you are responding to the change in your life and create a plan to help you get back in balance.

White Light: Bring the White Light through the crown of your head, into your feet, and into the Earth. It is a steady stream and you feel safe, comfortable, and at peace.

Visualization: Imagine that you are in water like a stream, lake, ocean, or wherever you see yourself when you close your eyes.

Imagine a raft. Where are you in relation to the raft? Are you on it? Is it on a boat nearby and you are struggling to stay afloat in the water? Are you on the raft but panicking? Are you clinging onto your raft, are you struggling in big waves, or perhaps you are floating on your raft and smiling? However you are responding on your raft is how you are responding to this change right now.

Look at your surroundings in the visualization. Is the water smooth or rough? Are there rocks in the water or near you? Are you stuck or going with the flow?

What is happening in the sky? Is it peaceful or cloudy? What is happening around you? Where is the White Light? Where is your support?

Letting go: Intuitively check in and ask what can you do to feel calm, balanced, and at peace in this exercise? Imagine letting any tension, frustration, and hopelessness disappear up into the Universe. Surrender this situation to the Universe. Know that the Universe is love and support.

White Light: Bring the White Light through your body, into your feet, and into the Earth. Imagine that you are sitting peacefully on the raft or that you feel peaceful in this situation. If you cannot, then do some more letting go. When you are finished, bring the White Light through your body, onto the raft, and into the water.

Mantra: Say, "All is well. The Universe supports me. Everything works out in the best way possible for everyone involved."

Is there anything else you should take away with you from this visualization? When you are finished, open your eyes.

Remember, how you saw yourself in this visualization is how you are responding to this change. If you are scared, you will attract more experiences to you to help you overcome your fears. Let your fears go. If you are calm, you will feel good and attract more of that to you.

The key is to be aware of how you are feeling. If you feel in any way that you are not in a calm, balanced place, let go of what is keeping you from that state of being.

Everything Works Out Perfectly

You are constantly learning and experiencing the things you are here to experience. The hardest part is often not the change itself, but the fear of the unknown. The actual change is freeing; it allows you to move forward in your life and onto the next experience.

The unknown seems scary, especially if you are waiting for the other shoe to drop. However, if you remember that you are always supported by the Universe, everything always works out. Nothing bad has to happen. The other shoe does not have to drop.

The "Everything Works Out Exercise," will help you find peace with all the craziness happening during change. The vision or image of yourself in your future that you see intuitively in this exercise is real. Focus on this vision or image to remind yourself that everything works out perfectly and that all is well. Note: You are not visualizing what you would like to see or your preferred possible outcomes. Instead, intuitively look for an image to help you through this change.

Remember this vision of you at the end of this major change whenever you start to worry about how things will work out. You will find that it brings you comfort and peace. Use this vision to help you calm any irrational or negative thinking your mind comes up with in the moment. Everything always works out perfectly, you just have to let it!

Everything Works Out Exercise

Use the image and the feelings you discover with this exercise to help you remember that this change does have an end and purpose in the big puzzle of life.

White Light: Bring the White Light through the crown of your head, into your feet, and into the Earth. It is a steady stream and you feel safe, comfortable, and at peace.

Visualization: Close your eyes. Intuitively imagine yourself at a time in your future when you are past this change (five years from now, ten years from now, or even later if that is what you see), and you feel happy, calm, and at peace.

Notice: What is happening around you? How do you feel now that you are past this change? What should you remember from this visualization to help you through this change?

Tips: If you find yourself having a hard time doing this exercise, do some letting go and try again later. The purpose of this is to help you know that everything works out, that whatever you are going through does have an ending. You are looking for an image of you being happy and when you see it, you take a mental picture of it. Then you use that image to combat any worry or negativity you are experiencing in the present. Do not come up with possibilities, plans, or focus on how this works out. Simply look for a time when this change is over and you are happy and at peace.

White Light: When you are finished, bring the White Light through your body, into your feet, and into the Earth. Open your eyes when you are ready.

Remember that you saw yourself being happy, calm, and at peace, so you know that everything works out. Again, it may not be how you think it should work out or how you try to make it work out, but it will work out in the best way possible for you and everyone involved. Whenever you start to feel overwhelmed, stressed, or fearful that things are not going to work out, do some letting go and then focus on the image and feelings from this visualization. You know that everything works out because you saw it being okay in this visualization. This will help you focus on the present moment instead of any worries or fears.

You may find that for each change you have a different visualization or one visualization for most changes. Perhaps you have a peaceful visualization or image that helps you through this change and several other changes. There is no right or wrong, just what supports you is what you are supposed to see.

You are Always Supported

You are supported at all times. No matter what hole, slippery slope, or darkness you may feel you are in, it is an illusion. You know this to be true, because you can feel the darkness and negativity disappear when you let it go and surround yourself in White Light. Anything that is not of love is not real. It is an illusion. Albeit, a powerful illusion at times, but you give that illusion power and you can take that power away.

Even if you feel like you are surrounded completely in darkness with no way out, remember, it is an illusion. Instead, look for the speck or sliver of light, it is always there. White Light conquers all. Use this exercise to show you how you are being supported right now.

Finding the Light Exercise

Always look for the speck of light when you feel lost or hopeless, it is always there. You are always supported by the Universe.

White Light: Bring the White Light through the crown of your head, into your feet, and into the Earth. It is a steady stream and you feel safe, comfortable, and at peace.

Visualization: Imagine that you are in a cave or another place that does not have a lot of light. Remember you are safe and supported.

All the darkness you feel (irritation, frustration, or negative thoughts), is in the air, but it is not your focus at first. Instead, look for the White Light that is shining through a hole or crack in the cave. You may even see the White Light at the end of a tunnel. Focus on the White Light, walk towards it, and let the White Light flow through your body.

Letting go: Let go of the darkness that you brought in with you. Then let go of any darkness or negativity surrounding you in your current situation. Let it all go. Imagine it disappearing into a speck of pepper and vanishing in the White Light.

White Light: Focus on the White Light and know, "I am safe. I am supported. I am well."

Open your eyes when you are ready. Where is your speck of light at this time? What image will you use to remember that you are supported?

Chapter Reminders

Change itself is not good or bad, it simply is. How you respond to the change is what shapes your next moment. Be aware of what you are feeling and what you are putting out to the Universe.

Your life is full of change! Most changes are so insignificant that you do not notice them. Sometimes, you will experience a change that is so intense, it makes your previously thought big changes look small. Small and big changes prepare you for life-altering changes. Typically you have multiple changes happening at a time and you go from one change to the next without skipping a beat.

Becoming aware of your energy in change is the key to how you experience this change in your life. What you focus on is what you create whether you are aware of what you are creating or not. Let go of the fear and trust that everything works out perfectly. Use your visualizations to help you remember this.

3 – Your Role in Change

Life is a process. At all times you are creating your reality whether you are aware of what you are creating or not. The more aware you are of what you are creating, the more you go with the flow. The less aware you are, the more you may find yourself struggling through this change.

In every change you have a role. Knowing what role you resonate with will help you understand why you are responding the way you are during each change. Then you can decide if what you are doing is supporting you or making this change harder than it has to be for you.

Your life is a master plan with flexibility. There are things that you are here to experience no matter what, and things that you may not end up experiencing in this life. Knowing which role scenario you are relating to and how you are creating this change in your life can make this process much easier.

Role Scenarios

Every change has a purpose. Sometimes, you know what that purpose is and sometimes you know pieces, but you cannot see the whole puzzle until long after it is done. In the end, everything always works out exactly as it should. When you feel out of balance, check in and see what role scenario you are resonating with at that time.

Once you know what role you have chosen for this change, then you can consciously be aware of how you respond to it.

There is no good or better role scenario, it is just a way to help explain what and how you are feeling in your life right now. When you are going through any change, you are a part of one of the following role scenarios: Bystander, Active Participant, or Active Participant that Lost Control.

Bystander

As a bystander, you may not feel like you have control over what is happening. Perhaps you feel as if you are a passenger being forced down a certain road and all you can do is hold on as tight as you can. You do not think you chose this change, nor do you think it should be happening.

In this scenario, you do not think you had a choice and you have lost control. You may even think you are a victim (even though you are not). This may not make sense to you in this moment, but at some level, you did choose this change. Somehow this change is going to help you have an experience you would like to have in this life.

Active Participant

As an active participant, you decide to make this change

consciously or you know a change is going to happen and you are willing to make this change happen. Sometimes, it goes well, sometimes it does not. Either way, you are okay with the process because you know you created it at some level.

Perhaps you can remember the thoughts and intentions that started this change. Maybe you knew this change was coming and you embraced it, focusing on the positive aspects. Regardless of how this change happens, you feel as if you are in control and all is well in your world, even if it does not appear that way to others. Often you go through this change feeling good about the process and your experience almost the whole time.

Active Participant that Lost Control

As an active participant that lost control, you will find that you have shifted roles in this change. Your excitement as an active participant has faded and now you feel stuck, trapped, and unsure of what to do next. You find yourself feeling like a Bystander. You do not know how this happened or how you could have prevented it, but you feel stuck and as if you are spinning out of control.

You will have moments where you can glimpse the light at the end of the tunnel, but then something throws you out of balance and everything seems dark and crazy again. Why did you decide to experience this change again? Do not worry; these are the experiences that really help you get back on track with your purpose. They just appear to have a backwards way of getting you there.

This role usually means that you are dealing with a life-altering change. You think you have a plan and you feel that you keep going with the flow, but this change seems endless. Now you are learning to trust and surrender so your focus can shift to getting back into balance. This experience with change will help you take surrendering, trusting, and staying in balance to a new level! In this place, it all works out better than you ever could have planned or imagined (more on this in chapter 5).

Which role scenario do you resonate with the most right now? Have you experienced parts of each scenario? How did you feel when each one was done? What pivotal moments and inspiration can you take from those experiences into this experience?

Ways You Create Change in Your Life

At some level you create this change in your life whether it is subconsciously, consciously, or it is a part of your master plan. Understanding how you are creating this change in your life can make this process much easier for you.

Your life is full of choices. Whether you are creating this change subconsciously or consciously, you are creating your life in line with your master plan for this experience. Learn to recognize the small road blocks as they appear in your life. Take time to understand why they are happening and what changes you should make. This can help prevent you from hitting a wall that forces you to a screeching halt.

Subconsciously

This means that you are not aware of what you are creating in your life. In this way, you feel like when something happens to you, it is a surprise that came out of nowhere. You feel that you had no control or power over it, it just happened. Perhaps you even feel like you are a victim.

Often times you are making an active choice to not be aware. For whatever reason, you do not want to be aware and you are okay feeling checked out. You may find yourself feeling numb or like a puppet just going through the daily motions of life. Sometimes, you may decide to check out for a part of the process and then check back in later.

At a subconscious level you are still a creator in your life, but you are not aware of what you are doing. In this awareness, it is as if you are driving a car while you are sleeping. You are still driving, you will probably crash, and then you will be forced to live consciously or be aware of where you are driving. This is a place that everyone experiences at some point.

Consciously

Consciously creating a change in your life means that you are aware of what you are creating. Perhaps you have been planning this event or maybe you know it is coming. Either way, you know it is happening and you have been preparing yourself for it.

You do not necessarily know the end result of the change, but you know that things are shifting. You may not be aware of everything that is going on, but you are awake, processing, and shifting with the road ahead of you.

Your Master Plan

Your life is a master plan that you are creating and following subconsciously and consciously. There are things you are here to experience, complete, and heal. This path is constantly shifting and changing based upon what you are doing (or not doing), and what you would like to be experiencing. Your master plan is something you create before you are born into this experience.

There are some things that are set in stone. This means that these events will happen in your life one way or another. There is no way around them, although sometimes when or how they will happen is often changeable.

At the same time, your life is full of free will. This means there are a lot of different options you can choose at any time. Each choice you make affects what happens next. Just because you decided to experience something on your master plan does not mean you are going to experience it how you originally intended.

Your path in this life is often not simple to understand, nor is it something you will understand while it is happening. What you would like to understand is why this change is so hard and it feels like everything is falling apart. Chances are, you are not doing what you are here to do and you are experiencing the road blocks you set up to help you get back on track.

Your Path

Imagine your path in life. There is a main path or line that represents all the "big" things you are here to do. Along this path are all the things that you are going to experience; they are not negotiable. They are a part of your purpose and you will do these things because this is what you decided before you were born. If you do not, you may feel like you are off track, like things are falling apart, and you may feel confused about what to do next.

There are also smaller things you would like to experience

and heal in this life. These are smaller paths that branch off, and they are all bonus experiences not required by you in this life. Sometimes, the smaller paths off of the main path are simpler ways to do a "big" thing.

Often you will see small pieces of how things are connected at a time. Pieces will be revealed as they relate to what you are experiencing now, otherwise it is too overwhelming. Understanding that you created this path, with your specific "obstacles" helps you recognize what is going on before you hit a big wall. If you feel like you are hitting a big wall, now you know that it is time to do something else since what you have been doing is not working for you.

Obstacles on Your Path

You put obstacles on the path to help you get back on track when you are not doing what you are here to do. Your obstacles start off small and grow larger as you ignore them, until you can no longer ignore them. For example, your obstacles begin as small rocks, which become boulders, and they turn into concrete walls along your path forcing you to stop and find an alternate route.

Think about an example of what signals your body gives you when you do not get enough sleep. You are tired but you ignore it and keep going. This can lead to a headache, but you ignore it and do not rest. Your body is tired and would like rest, so it starts to ache with exhaustion and then you get sick, forcing you to stop and rest. Similarly, your path of change begins with small detours for you not making the change and the detours grow as you continue ignoring the change(s) you have to make in your life. Are you being punished? Absolutely not!

The Universe does not punish, it is truly here to support you. The only one that can punish you is you, and punishment is not necessary at any time. Remember, you are love. No experience is here to hurt you unless you choose for it to happen that way at some level. Even then, see if there is another way to experience that situation in a more supportive way. You create the obstacles in your life to help you get back on track. It really is that simple.

How does this work? Imagine that you are supposed to be doing something and you decide you are not going to do it. You feel the pull to make this change, but you ignore it. At this time, you will experience a rock in your path. It could manifest in any way, but typically you will not be getting something you think you want. As you continue to ignore this path that you are supposed to be on, you will hit a bigger obstacle. This will continue on until you do what you are supposed to be doing or until you are forced to stop and make the detour. At this point, it will feel like you hit a cement wall.

For example, perhaps you are staying at a job that is draining you, and you would like to leave but you feel you cannot, so you stay. This is like encountering a rock in your path. Then things will start happening slowly to help you leave. Perhaps the workplace gets hostile or unethical things are happening, but you stay and now you experience a bigger obstacle. Eventually, things keep happening until something bigger happens like not getting a promotion or raise you are supposed to get. Perhaps you leave by choice or something happens that pushes you out of that company, which feels like hitting a cement wall.

Obviously, the earlier you make the change, the easier the whole experience will be for you. The longer you wait and put off the change, the harder it feels emotionally and mentally. By waiting to make the change, you are not being punished. You are simply being pushed to make this change that you decided to make before you were born. Consider it a reminder that gets louder as you ignore it.

The moment you start to make the change you have been fighting or ignoring, you start to feel better instantly. This is no indication of how the rest of the change will go. Every experience you have is different depending on how and what you would like to experience from it. Asking the Universe for guidance when you do not know what to do is the most powerful way to course correct.

Guidance Exercise

Ask the Universe for guidance or next steps in this change.

White Light: Bring the White Light through the crown of your head, into your feet, and into the Earth. It is a steady stream and you feel safe, comfortable, and at peace.

Letting go: Imagine all the frustration, hopelessness, or aggravation you feel right now flowing out of your being and into the Universe or sky. Give it all away.

Then allow the White Light to flow through you again, and into the Earth. Know that the Universe is supporting you.

Visualization: Let the Universe help you with whatever is going on in your life in this moment. Remember, the Universe always supports you. Ask the Universe what you should be doing now or what your next steps are. You may hear, see, or know what your next steps are after asking this question.

Tips: If it does not come to you right away, what is keeping you from seeing what to do next? Is there more letting go to do? If you have anything else to let go of release it until you feel free and supported.

Then ask the Universe what you should be doing to help you get back on track. There is always something you can be doing, even if it is nurturing yourself or appreciating a break before the next thing comes into your life.

White Light: Bring the White Light through the crown of your head, into your feet, and into the Earth. It is a steady stream and you feel safe, comfortable, and at peace.

Open your eyes when you are ready.

Chapter Reminders

Remember that your role in this change shapes how you are experiencing it. If you feel like a bystander, you will feel powerless. However, if you feel like an active participant, you will feel empowered. However you feel about your role, is how you will respond. How do you feel about your role?

In every moment, you create your life either subconsciously or consciously. How do you think you are creating this change? Catch yourself when you start making important decisions without being aware of what you are doing. The more aware you are of what you are creating, the easier things will be for you in the long run. What can you do to feel more empowered and balanced in this moment?

Your life is a master plan that you created before you were born. Some obstacles you are here to experience and some are here to help you shift your current path, like a detour. Are there any obstacles on your path right now? If so, what should you be doing?

4 – Colors and Rainbows

You are naturally drawn to colors that will support you in each day and moment. Look at the colors you chose to wear in your outfit today. How do these colors make you feel? Do they feel nurturing and supportive? Perhaps you even see the color(s) you chose to wear today around you more than any other color. You may even feel like you are pulled to that color today every chance you get to pick something with a color in it. Sometimes, you may find that when you pick out an outfit to wear the night before, the next morning, you decide to wear a different color that feels better instead. At some level, you have been using colors subconsciously to support you all along.

Pastel colors, rainbows, and mantras will help support you when you feel like you can use a little extra help regaining your balance. Once you start using them, you will realize that you were using them subconsciously before, and it worked. Now you can benefit from them even more by using them consciously.

There are many different ways you can visualize colors to help you find peace no matter what you are experiencing in this process of change. At this point you are very familiar with White Light. White Light is a staple that you will always use to begin any energy work. Now you will learn how to use other colors and rainbows to help support your being.

Pastel Colors

White Light is always there. You are a part of the White Light, and White Light makes anything not of love (any darkness or negativity), disappear. By this point, you know how supported, balanced, and grounded you feel when you practice using the White Light. White Light reflects all the colors equally. However, you can use pastel colors to help and support your being in different ways and in different experiences.

The first color you always use is white. It grounds you and helps you create a safe space. Since the White Light reflects all of the colors equally that means all the colors are present. Sometimes, when you are bringing the White Light through your body, you will notice other colors mixed in there. It is okay to see the other colors, but the first color you always focus on is white. After you bring the white through, you can focus on the other color(s) you are seeing or are drawn to use.

If you have a lot going on right now or if you have done a lot of letting go, you will feel a pull to surround yourself in a specific color. Chances are, you are wearing that color now and you have been using that color whenever you can. You may reach for a pen, marker, sticky note, or even a mug that color. You probably even notice that color as you are out and about, as if that color is everywhere you look, a little miracle to support you in your journey today.

The pastel colors can flow through your body just like the White Light or you can use them in a specific area of your body. There is no right or wrong, just what works for you in that moment. However, if you see dark colors like red, navy blue, forest green, etc., this is a way for you to know that you have some healing to do in that area. You may see this color once or you may see it for a small period of time. This is not good or bad, just a sign for you to pay attention to this area and the color your body would like in that area at this moment.

If you see black, gray, or smoke, there is letting go to do immediately. Just push that energy out of your body wherever you see it. Then fill it with White Light where those colors were.

Use the pastel colors to nurture and support your body. You may use different colors in different areas. Sometimes, it is helpful to know what a color means to help you heal something that you have been subconsciously storing in your body. Other times, knowing what a color means may put you in more of an analytical place. Do not spend time analyzing the color, let this be more of an intuitive process and shift your focus to letting the color support you. Use the color you feel a pull to use where it will support your being.

Life is all about going with the flow and doing what you intuitively know will support you. You do not have to put these colors where you think they should go or where you have read they should go. Instead, let the colors tell you where they belong at this moment in your body. You may find yourself using one color or many; do what supports you in this moment.

Typical meanings for pastel colors as they support you:

Pink: Love, pamper, and support for that area

Blue: Peace, calm, neutralizes your energy in that area

Green: Nurturing, abundance

Orange: Support after an intense emotional release

Yellow: Rejuvenates you, raises your energy level when you are tired or low energy

Purple: Supports your energy at a spiritual level

Remember, this is just a generic guide for the meaning of the pastel colors you will see or feel. You may use colors in a different way or they may have a different meaning to you when you are using them. Always trust how you are getting to use the colors for yourself and use them that way.

Gold and Silver Sparkles

Although these are not pastel colors, they can be mixed with the pastel colors to help you clear out an area and reprogram it. They are very powerful, supportive, and healing.

If you see these, just let them do their work. If you do not see them, do not worry. Sometimes, you will see them, sometimes you will not. They will only be there if they are supposed to be there healing you.

Now that you know what the colors do, take a moment to practice the "Color Exercise." Let the White Light flow through you, and then use whatever colors pop into your mind.

Color Exercise

Use whatever colors you are guided to use to support your being. This is especially helpful to do if you feel overwhelmed, if you have just done a lot of letting go, or you could use come extra support.

White Light: Bring the White Light through the crown of your head, into your feet, and into the Earth. It is a steady stream and you feel safe, comfortable, and at peace.

Color visualization: Imagine the color that supports you the most right now in the area of your body that it should be in.

Tips: For example, what color would your hips like to have? Imagine that color coming in from behind you, through that area of your body, and out the front of your body.

You can also imagine the colors traveling through your being from your crown, to your feet, and into the Earth.

If you cannot see the color, imagine it being wrapped around you like a blanket. Then fill that part of your being with that color. Imagine the blanket spreading the color through that area as if it is heat from the blanket.

What color should you use in your:

Head

Throat

Shoulders

Chest and back

Stomach

Hips

Thighs

Knees

Lower legs

Feet

Into the Earth

Use whatever colors you see. If you feel any tension or see any darkness or energetic blocks, simply let them go. Surround them with the color you are seeing and push them out of your body. Remember, it is okay to see more than one color in an area. Sometimes, you may see multiple colors.

Closing: Let whatever color you intuitively see in this moment flow through your entire being. You feel nurtured, supported, and pampered.

White Light: Bring the White Light through your being and into the Earth.

Open your eyes when you are ready.

You can use colors on their own or in conjunction with other exercises in this book. Always do what will support you the most in that moment.

Letting Go with Colors Exercise

Use colors to help you release whatever you are holding onto. This exercise is typically reserved for when it is hard to let go of any tension or darkness you are seeing in your body.

White Light: Bring the White Light through the crown of your head, into your feet, and into the Earth. It is a steady stream and you feel safe, comfortable, and at peace.

Color visualization: Imagine the color that supports you the most in this moment surrounding the darkness or negativity in your body and pushing it out. Bring the color into your body from behind you and let the color surround any darkness or negativity (anything that is not of love or that you are letting go of), and push it out of your body. Let the color expand through that whole area until you feel it flow through the front of your body.

Check in: Check in with yourself and see if there is more letting go to do in that area. If there is, do it. If not, then bring the White Light back through your whole body from the crown of your head, down into your feet, and into the Earth.

Open your eyes when you are ready.

Surround that area of your body in that color for a few days. You may wear that color, put stones of the same color on or near that area, or surround yourself with things that are that color. You can write an "I am" statement on a sticky note that color and pin it to your clothes or somewhere you will see it often for the next few days. Do what supports you and feels right to your being.

Rainbows

Rainbows are literally what you see on a rainy day. They are pastel colors that nurture, support, and align your whole being (body, mind, and spirit). Rainbows are not one or two colors like pastel colors, the rainbow colors will appear together.

Visually you will see each color of the rainbow individually come through your body (one color after another), or you will see an actual rainbow flow through you. Either way, it is supporting your being in the best way for you in that moment.

Rainbows for Support

The rainbow is not necessarily something that you will use on a daily basis like the White Light unless you are going through a lot of changes. Every day you can find at least a speck of light poking through clouds, if not more, in the sky. However, you do not see a rainbow every day. In nature, you typically see a rainbow in the sky after a storm. The colors are reflections of light that brighten up the stormy sky. Just as you do not see a rainbow often, you will find you do not use rainbows as often as White Light.

Energetically, the rainbow is used to realign your being; especially when you are feeling overwhelmed or your body has done a lot of letting go. Basically, you will use it when you feel you can use a little extra support and alignment. Usually when it feels like you have been through a rocky patch or storm in your life, it is time to use a rainbow in your visualizations. You will notice that from this point on in the book that some of the exercises end with a rainbow and not White Light. Always end your sessions with White Light, a pastel color, or a rainbow. Use whatever you see that will support you at that time.

You will feel energized, aligned, and purposeful after you do the "Rainbow Exercise." If you do use the rainbow in a single area, when that area feels complete, make sure to bring the rainbow through your whole being, just like White Light.

You will know when you should add a rainbow to any of the work you are doing. Always trust what you intuitively know will support your being and do it.

Rainbow Exercise

Use the rainbow to support and realign your being when there is a lot going on in your life or after an intense letting go session.

White Light: Bring the White Light through the crown of your head, into your feet, and into the Earth. It is a steady stream and you feel safe, comfortable, and at peace.

Rainbow visualization: Imagine a rainbow of pastel colors flowing through your body. You may see the colors individually, flow through one color at a time until you have gone through the rainbow, or all at once like a rainbow you can see in the sky.

The rainbow begins at the crown of your head, flows through your body, into your feet, and into the Earth. The colors are pastel and each color is equally flowing into you.

Just be: Sit there and watch this rainbow flowing through your being for a few minutes. Relax and if you feel any fears or negativity in your body, let them go, and replace them with the colors of the rainbow.

Open your eyes when you are ready.

Rainbows for Abundance

Abundance is more than money, although when you are dealing with big and life-altering changes, this may be your focus. However, abundance is love, relationships, opportunities, support, and basically anything that the Universe is sending your way and to others through you.

Use the rainbow to help realign your energy when you have a lot of fears that are out of control about abundance. When your relationships and finances are affected, any chaos preventing abundance will usually get your immediate attention. You can bring more abundance into your life during change by being aware of what you are blocking and what you are allowing into your life.

The Universe will always give you what you are supposed to have. You just have to let it in and not block it or stop it by saying you have enough. There really is plenty for everyone. Let abundance flow into your life without saying what abundance means or what you think you "need." Instead, receive what you are supposed to be receiving. Let abundance flow into your being and into everyone around you.

Notice, there is no asking for anything in the "Rainbow Abundance Exercise." You are trusting that whatever you are supposed to have, you will have. Let go of anything blocking the abundance from flowing into your being.

Rainbow Abundance Exercise
Consciously let abundance flow into you and let go of anything that is blocking it.

White Light: Bring the White Light through the crown of your head, into your feet, and into the Earth. It is a steady stream and you feel safe, comfortable, and at peace.

Let go: Let go of any fears, limitations, or things that are blocking you at this moment. Release them to the Universe, push them out of your body, and then bring the White Light through your body again.

Rainbow visualization: Imagine a rainbow of pastel colors flowing into the front of your chest and into your being. The colors are pastel and each color is equally flowing into you at the same time in the same amount, just like a rainbow.

Allow the energy to flow into your chest until it feels complete.

Tips: If you find yourself stopping the energy or feeling like it is too much, you have more letting go to do. Let go of whatever is limiting you and then imagine the rainbow flowing into your chest again.

Share abundance with others: Once you feel complete, imagine the energy flowing into the environment around you. You can imagine yourself in nature, in a space you like to visit in meditation, or in the "real" world. Let the rainbow flow through you and to wherever it is supposed to go until it feels complete.

Open your eyes when you are ready.

"I am" Statements, Mantras, and Colors

Pastel colors and rainbows are nurturing and supportive. Often no words have to be used with them. You just see the colors, let them do their work, and you feel great. Sometimes, you will find that it is helpful for you to have something for your mind to focus on like an "I am" statement or mantra like "all is well," with the colors.

"I am" statements or mantras can be very supportive with colors when you have done a lot of energy work. For example, you can use this combination after an intense letting go session or when you are changing an old, powerful, thought pattern. Typically, you do this combination for about three consecutive days or until you feel something else will support you. Always, check in intuitively and see if you should still be doing this exercise or if another exercise would support you more.

There are several "I am" statements to help you through this transition. Use what helps you the most and what you connect with the most. Here are some "I am" and mantra suggestions:

"I am love. I am light. I am safe. I am whole."

"I am peace. I am calm."

"All is well. All is as it should be."

"Love flows through my being. Only love remains."

"Everything works out in the best way possible for everyone involved."

"The Universe supports me and I support the Universe."

Which statement do you connect most with right now? If you do not connect with one of these suggestions, feel free to make your own or to make your own combination. You have to say something you connect with and that supports your current situation or it will not work.

Remember, you are a being of light and love, focus on the positive. If you cannot, then do some letting go. Make your statements and mantras as concise as possible. This will make it easier to remember and you will find that you say it more often. The simpler your "I am" statement or mantra is, the better!

Color and "I am" Exercise

Use a pastel color visualization with an "I am" or mantra to support your being after an intense letting go session.

White Light: Bring the White Light through the crown of your head, into your feet, and into the Earth. It is a steady stream and you feel safe, comfortable, and at peace.

Visualization: Imagine the pastel color or rainbow, whatever supports you the most right now. You can imagine it filling all of your body like the White Light or a specific area. Do what works for you in this moment.

Words: Use the mantra or "I am" statement that supports you in this moment.

Imagine the words blending with the energy of the pastel color in your body and into the Earth. Know that you are nurturing and supporting your being. Stay in this place until you feel complete.

Open your eyes when you are ready.

Chapter Reminders

The pastel colors, rainbows, and colors with words are important tools that you will see incorporated into other exercises. Always make sure you are doing what supports your being the most in this moment. You always know what to do, make sure you are doing it and not just thinking about it.

Always use White Light to begin any energy work you are going to do. White Light helps you center and ground yourself. White Light is a reflection of all the colors equally and you are the White Light.

Once in a while, you may notice another color coming in strongly as you bring the White Light through your body. Sometimes, you will feel a pull to use a color other than white. If this happens, it is okay. Finish bringing the White Light through. Always balance your body first with White Light, then you can shift your focus and support your body with this other color.

Colors are nurturing and supportive. Pastels can be used alone, or with "I am" statements or mantras to support you. You will see or feel the colors and when you do, make sure you use them. Rainbows help you realign. You will see or feel all the colors of the rainbow. Use rainbows for support or when you are doing abundance exercises.

5 – Control, Surrender, and Trust

Part of your journey is learning what you can control and what you cannot control during change. Change is like a roller coaster with its ups and downs, making it important for you to be aware of what is going on and how you are responding.

Depending on what the change is in your life determines how much fear is running the show instead of trust. Smaller changes in your life are easier to trust and go with the flow since there is less risk, and in the end, less growth on your part. Life-altering changes are unknown territories. They invoke more fear because they require more risk and trust over a longer period of time.

Regardless of the types of change you are experiencing right now, they are affecting your relationships. Your relationship with yourself, your significant other, your family, your work, and your finances, are just some of the things you are trying to balance and figure out. Often, the more personal and life-altering the change, the more you grasp for control. Then, the more stressed you become trying to figure out how to control it all. Any substantial change dealing with your relationships, especially financially, is going to feel more intense because it feels as if you have more to lose. For example, a divorce is harder than a break up, and a job loss is harder than willingly changing jobs in the same industry.

What is giving you energy and what is draining you? How do you get back to a place of peace and balance? During big changes in your life, it becomes essential to become aware of where you are putting your energy and how you are using it.

Understanding what you do and do not control will help you know where to put your energy. Knowing when to surrender and trust so you can let a miracle happen will also make your process much easier.

What You Do Control

As powerless as you may feel at times during any big change, there are many things you do control and have the ability to change. By knowing what you have control over, helps you move more fluidly through the process. Some things you have control over are: your thoughts, your words, your actions, your space, and letting go of anything that is no longer serving you.

Your Thoughts

Become aware of your thoughts. Thoughts become your reality so be aware of what you are creating. What are you focusing on in this moment? Ask yourself this question when you find yourself starting to worry during this change. Once you start worrying, you will find yourself creating the very things you were worried about happening. Catch yourself before your worry shifts your focus, often in a downward spiral.

If you focus on being grateful instead of worrying about what is coming next, you will immediately feel more calm and peaceful. Being grateful brings you into this moment. Worrying does not help you in any way; all it does is create more worry. Remember, what you focus on is what you create. Worry brings more worry and gratitude brings more experiences for you to be grateful for. Which would you rather have more of in your life?

Analyzing what has happened puts you in the past, and trying to predict what will happen next forces you into a fictitious future. Being grateful gives you back control and puts you in the present moment, where you have power. In order to focus on the present moment where you have power, you have to let go of whatever keeps pulling you into the past or future.

Present Moment Exercise

Bring your attention and energy into the present moment when you are worried or stressed.

Stop the thought: Imagine a stop sign or red light halting the thought immediately, or freeze the thought on ice. Then push the thought away. You can imagine the thought turning into a speck of pepper and disappearing into the Universe, or you can imagine pushing it out of your mind and up into the sky.

White Light: Bring the White Light through the crown of your head, into your feet, and into the Earth. It is a steady stream and you feel safe, comfortable, and at peace.

Be grateful: Once you feel the White Light flowing through your body, it is time to be grateful. What are you grateful for in this moment?

Tips: Whatever first pops into your mind is your focus and it can be anything! It can be the chair you are sitting in, it can be a smell in the air, being able to take a deep breath, a loved one, an experience you recently had, or literally whatever you are truly grateful for in this moment. If you think of something and try to pretend that is what you are grateful for, it will not work. You have to be grateful for whatever it is that is popping into your mind.

If you find yourself struggling to find something you are grateful for, there is letting go to do. What are you holding on to that is preventing you from experiencing joy? What are you afraid of? Are you afraid that if you appreciate something it will disappear? Perhaps you believe you do not deserve something to be grateful for? Regardless of what is preventing you from being grateful release

it, do your "I am" statements, and then your, "I am grateful for
_____."

Visualization: Imagine that what you are grateful for is flowing through your body, just like the White Light is. "I am grateful for_____." Let this grateful energy flow through your being with White Light.

Open your eyes when you are ready.

In every moment, there is always something to be grateful for. Try practicing this throughout the day. Again, do not just go through the motions, really do it.

Your Words

Your thoughts become your words, so you can see how powerful they are. Obviously, words mean what they say they mean. Want means you want it and you do not have it, nor can you get it. Same thing goes for words like need, desire, and wish.

However, when you are in the chaos of change, the words you may use are: "This is helpless. I am stuck. Nothing is changing. I give up," or fill in the blank with what you are saying to yourself now: "_____." Whether you say these words to yourself silently in your head or out loud, the end result is the same. You are creating your reality. Now erase all those words because that is not what you are going to create.

If things seem hard, instead of focusing on how hard they are (and creating more "hard" times or experiences), focus on what is working well. There is always something working, something in your life that is not broken. Find what it is in that moment and focus on it. Put all your energy in that moment into feeling what is working well. Even if it is your lungs being able to breathe or your stomach digesting the food you ate earlier, it is still something working during this change in your life.

Focus on what is Working Exercise

Whenever you start to think that things are not working, remember to do this exercise and focus on what is working well in your life right now.

White Light: Bring the White Light through the crown of your head, into your feet, and into the Earth. It is a steady stream and you feel safe, comfortable, and at peace.

Let go: Let go of whatever you think is not working. Surrender it to the Universe. Imagine handing it over to the Universe and giving it all away. Trust and know that it will work out in the best way possible for everyone involved.

Tips: You may have some letting go to do to surrender the

situation and to trust the Universe to take care of it. If you do have letting go to do, know that it involves your ego. Sometimes, your ego thinks it has more control than it really does. (In this chapter there is a whole section on surrendering to help you with this.)

Visualization: Focus on one thing that is working in your life in this moment. What is it?

How does this make you feel (happy, at peace, or calm)?

White Light: Bring the energy of that feeling through your whole body. Let it flow through your body just like the White Light and with the White Light.

Open your eyes when you are ready.

Your Actions

In every moment, you have complete control of what you are doing. This is especially evident in your body's actions. If you are angry or frustrated, you have a choice. Do you throw something violently across the room or do you decide to go for a walk and do some letting go instead? Perhaps you can pause before you do what you always do and see if that action makes sense in this situation.

Pay attention to your actions when you are around other people. This is not a way to judge yourself, but a way to look objectively at what you are doing through other people's eyes. Notice how other people are responding to your actions. If just one person is having a response and no one else, perhaps that situation has nothing to do with you. However, if you find yourself eliciting the same response from numerous people, take a look at what you are doing and change it if it is not working for you anymore.

Everything has a time and place, including your behavior. What will help you get back in balance? Sometimes, doing what you always do just creates more chaos, something you do not have to have in your life. This next exercise is one that you can practice doing in charged situations. Instead of reacting and being sorry later, try pausing before you respond. You will find it is easier to handle a situation from a calm perspective, and after you will feel better too. If you are happy with how you handle a situation, there is no judging or over-analyzing. You can simply let the situation be and move on to the next thing.

Pause then Respond Exercise

Instead of just responding, pause first. Decide what the best use of your energy is before you take action.

White Light: Bring the White Light through the crown of your head, into your feet, and into the Earth. It is a steady stream and you feel safe, comfortable, and at peace.

Let go: Let go of whatever is frustrating you or causing you unease in this moment. You can do this by taking a few deep breaths. Breathe in White Light; exhale whatever is setting you off.

Pause: Before you respond, decide if this is even something you would like to, or should, engage in. In our society, it seems like you have to respond quickly, but pausing first allows you to respond in the best way for you at that moment. This will also prevent you from being upset about acting too quickly or hastily, and then apologizing later.

If you engage: Ask yourself what is the best way for you to respond for everyone involved? What is the most helpful? Do it and keep checking in with yourself to make sure that this is the best way to respond.

If you do not engage: Imagine pushing the energy from this situation away from your being. Do not allow it near you energetically. Instead, give it back to the person(s) giving it to you. This does not have to be done in a mean or negative way; you are just simply deciding not to engage. You do not have to take on this energy being given to you by someone else. Let them keep their energy and you keep yours.

White Light: Bring the White Light back through your body. If you feel there is any letting go to do, do it, and then bring the White Light through your body again.

Your eyes will probably be open for all of this, since you may be doing it in front of other people, but if they are not, open them.

Be aware of where you are putting your energy after this experience. What other exercises can you do to support your being in this moment?

Your Space

You have complete control of the energy you allow in your space, whether that is a space in your house, at work, or in your car. You are responsible for the energy where you are. If you do not like it, change it. Push out any negativity and bring the White Light into the space.

If the space is not yours to clear, any energy you remove will probably keep coming back. When this happens, your focus shifts from clearing the space to doing what you can do to be comfortable in that space.

For example, if you are at someone else's house and you notice that the space energetically feels negative or dirty; you often cannot clear it as they put that energy there. That person has to be ready for the space to be cleared or they will put the energy back.

Instead, be aware of your energy. Bring the White Light through you and do not pick up on any of the energy in the space. If you find that too hard to do, then do not go to that space until you can do it. However, if you do have to be in that space, remember that you can be anywhere. You are always safe in the White Light no matter what is going on around you.

Clearing Your Space Exercise

Use this exercise to clear energy, negative energy, or spirits out of a space that you have permission to clear. This space can be a building, a room, land, or whatever you feel a pull to energetically clear.

White Light: Bring the White Light through the crown of your head, into your feet, and into the core of the Earth. It is a steady stream and you feel safe, comfortable, and at peace. Say, "I am love. I am light. I am safe. I am whole."

Center of room: Begin by standing as close as you can to the middle of the space that you would like to energetically clear.

Spirits or Energies: If you feel there are any spirits or energies in the space, release them first. If not, go to "Energetically clearing your space."

Imagine a beam of White Light and let the spirit(s) go into it. Spirits are typically ready to leave if you are aware of them. They typically go into the light without any issue because they are ready to return to the light.

Also imagine putting any energies into the light. Sometimes, you have to mean business and be forceful, especially if you are dealing with an energy that you allowed to attach to you to "help you." Energies disappear in the light since they are an absence of love; they are an illusion.

If spirits or energies choose not to go into the light, that is fine. Tell them silently or out loud that they can no longer stay in this space. Then imagine using the White Light to push them out and away from that space.

Tips: Imagine putting whatever spirits or energies you are seeing, sensing, hearing, or feeling into the White Light to release it. You do not have to know who the spirit is, or what energy you are clearing.

A good practice is to let go of anything in a space that is not of love. Energy is either love or it is not. Remember anything not of love is an illusion, and it will disappear in the White Light.

Energetically clearing your space: Focus your attention on the space to be cleared. Notice where the energy is, usually it is in one part of the space. You may feel, see, or know that it is there. Once you start clearing the space, you may find other areas to clear.

White Light: With your hands, bring the White Light through the crown of your head, into your feet, and into the core of the Earth. Then use your hands as a wand to put the White Light into the space and push the negativity, or darkness out of the area. Slowly spin around. Start at the very bottom of the space with the White Light, and imagine any negativity or darkness is disappearing or being pushed up and far from the space by the light.

It is as if you are sweeping the energy away with your hands and it never enters your being. You can imagine it leaving as smoke, disappearing into a speck of pepper, and then disappearing up in the sky or into the Universe. After the base of the space is done, do the middle, and then the top.

Tips: Release the energy quickly; do not hold onto any of it. Energy can move as fast as you can snap your fingers, so do not feel like you have to spend a lot of time moving it. You are cleaning the space just like you would sweep a room in your house. You do not have to know what happened there or why. Just let all the negativity leave as it does not belong there anymore.

White Light: When you feel that the whole space is done (should take a few minutes), bring the White Light into the space from the bottom to the top. You can imagine starting at the core of the Earth and bringing the light all the way up into the Universe. Imagine every crevice being filled with the White Light.

Then bring the White Light into the space again from the sky to below the space. Imagine the White Light in large beams of light and know that it is covering the whole area, pushing out any residual darkness or negativity.

Bring the White Light through your body, into your feet, and into the Earth. Say, "I am love. I am light. I am safe. I am whole."

If your eyes were closed, open your eyes when you are ready.

Tips for Clearing a Space

As with any energy releasing, you may notice the energy trying to come back. This happens most often within the first three days, and at night. In the day it is easier to see the light and at night it is easier to see darkness. Once the energy knows you really do mean business and you are not going to let it in, it will go away. If you feel the energy come back, just push it away with your hands or visually in your mind, and then bring the White Light back through you and through the space. At night, you can also turn on a light and you will feel it disappear. Once you turn on the light, bring the White Light through your being, say your mantra, and know that you are safe.

You can clear the energy out of a space as often as you feel you should. However, you should find yourself doing it less and less, especially as you become more aware of your energy and what you are allowing into the space. You may find yourself doing a quick energy clearing the first few days, then once a week, and then monthly to keep the space clear until you no longer feel it has to be done.

Right after you clear a space, you can put special crystals, stones, or objects in that space as a reminder to you that this space is clear and safe. Remove the items when you no longer feel they have to be in that space.

If you put any crystals, stones, or objects in the space to help you remember it is clear, it is important to energetically clean those items weekly or more often. You will know it is time to clean them when they feel dirty, or when your clean hands feel dirty when you touch them. You can bring the White Light through your being and then hold the items and imagine the White Light cleaning the items. You can also rinse them in cold water until they feel clean, and then put them in the morning sun or under a full moon to dry and charge, depending on the energy you would like to give the item. The sun and moon charge crystals and stones differently, so research what will support you most, and do it.

What You Do Not Control

Sometimes, you may find yourself trying to control things that you have absolutely no control over. This is especially true when you feel like you have lost control and you are trying to grab onto something to help you feel like you do have control. What you will find is that when you try to control things that are not yours to control, life gets a lot more complicated.

When and How Life Happens

You are a creator in your life, but your life is bigger than you as it involves many others. Believing that you have complete control over everything around you is a romantic notion that your ego tells you, and your mind would love to make happen. Life is about going with the flow, not controlling everything around you. Remember you are here for the experiences, not a lack of them.

Making Things Happen

How you have experienced change before is no indicator of how you will be experiencing it this time. This is a new moment, a different time, a different experience, and you are a different person, so it will probably require some new approaches. If you are implementing your plan without roadblocks, keep going. However, if you find you are stuck and you keep hitting roadblocks, perhaps it is time to change your approach.

Try not to force things to happen simply because you believe they should be happening in a specific way. It may seem like that works once in a while, but things happen because they are supposed to happen. Not necessarily because you tried to make it happen. Thinking you have that much control is really just a power trip for your ego. Unfortunately, that power trip slows things down for you and makes things more complicated. Adding complication to a big or life-altering change is not the best thing for you to do, especially if you are feeling stuck.

Of course you should have plans and goals, but they are most successful when you surrender the *how,* and flow with the Universe. Remember, you only see a small part of the bigger puzzle. Getting frustrated and upset because you think you know *how* things should be happening (because you have a detailed plan), is not often the best approach.

Sometimes, you can visualize the end result and you find yourself taking whatever practical steps it should take to get there. Yet, when you do the practical steps, things are just not working out according to plan. You revise, you put the new plan into action, and random things are making everything fall apart. Everything feels like it is crumbling and you wonder what happened. In this situation, things shifted. The best way to flow in this situation is to check in and see what the new plan is since the old plan is simply not happening no matter what you do.

Life is a process bigger than you as it involves billions of people and their processes too. Things will happen when they are supposed to. Of course, there are things that you are supposed to do to help those things happen, and there are times when it seems you do not have to do anything. If you see a piece of the puzzle, do what you are supposed to with that information. Let go of your frustration when you are waiting for the next piece to fall into place and things will be so much easier.

When you Feel Done, Surrender Instead

The absolute worst thing you can say or scream is, "I am done." Unfortunately, when you say this, it does not stop or shorten the process. This is not surrendering and trusting that everything will work out. Your statement means that you do not "want" to do whatever that experience is anymore. "I am done," means that you are giving up, you cannot do this, or you do not want to do this. You will find that you will stay in that space until you can find a way to complete the experience. This is not to punish you or harm you in anyway. There is no quitting an experience simply because you feel like it, as I am sure you have discovered. You are having that experience to heal something and it will be done when that part is healed.

At some level you chose to have this experience at this time in your life. Instead of trying to control the situation or feeling done, try surrendering it to the Universe. Instead of saying, "I am done," say, "I give this situation to the Universe. I surrender this situation so it can work out in the best way possible for everyone involved. I am peace." You will probably have to let go of the beliefs and expectations that were holding you trapped, and then you can allow this new "I am" statement to flow through you.

Surrender sounds like it is a complete loss of control, but it really is the opposite. The moment you stop letting your ego or mind run the show, the Universe is able to flow in to support you. By releasing your expectations and beliefs on how something should be, you allow in more possibilities. The limitations you put on yourself are then gone and anything is possible. Things always work out better when you step out of the way and let them happen. Instead of worrying about how life is going to happen, focus on what is working, what is flowing, and what is going well.

Surrender the situation to the Universe and start going with the flow. Check in with yourself and see what letting go you have to do. What exercises will support you right now? There is an exercise on surrendering coming up at the end of the chapter to support you as well.

Other People

You are surrounded by people throughout much of your day. Whether you are driving your car, in a store, going for a walk, or in your house with family, there are people all around you with their energy.

Sometimes, the people that surround you nurture you and support you, sometimes they do not. You may find that you are trying to get people to do what you would like them to do. Perhaps they are trying to get you to do something that they would like you to do. At this point, you know that you do not control anyone other than yourself and they do not control you.

Think about a crying baby at a restaurant. The parents would love for the baby to be happy, but sometimes no matter what they do, they cannot make the baby happy. Eventually, they have to take the baby out of the restaurant so they can help the baby. However, there are still people from that experience that will only remember the crying baby that supposedly "ruined" their meal even hours after the dinner. You cannot control anyone other than yourself, nor can you control someone else's response to a situation. A crying baby can only ruin your meal if you let it by making it your focus.

Your job is to focus on your experience. You may be able to help others or bring them joy at times, but your focus is not making them happy. What are you supposed to be experiencing? How does this person help you experience that? If they are not helping you and they are only causing you more frustration, perhaps it is time to take a break from that person.

A break can offer you both time to course correct in a way you cannot if you are in constant contact. Distance makes the heart grow fonder, or it helps you realize that the relationship served its purpose and now it is time for both of you to move on. In the end, you do not have control over other people and you do not have to give them control over you. Instead, we have an impact on each other because we are all connected.

Is there a relationship in your life that is hurting you more than helping you at this time? Are you trying to control someone or is someone trying to control you? What will nurture, support, and get you back into balance in this moment?

Surrender and Trust

During change, control is something you are often grasping

for, but it is not necessarily what will help you when you cannot see everything that is in motion. Even if you think you know all the steps to take, you cannot control when a sudden detour is made. Think of a time in your life when you felt you were up against a wall, with no choice but to surrender the situation. What happened when you did that? How did things work out?

Surrendering is like a Hail Mary in a football game. Usually, when you think about surrendering, it is because you have tried every other possible solution and nothing is working. You throw a Hail Mary out to the Universe and hope for the best. While surrendering does work in this way, it also works when you do it before you get to that point of hopelessness.

You do not have to be at your weakest hour on your knees to surrender. On the contrary, when you do not know what to do in a situation, trust the Universe to help you through it. You are not done and throwing your arms up in the air frustrated. Instead, you are calmly asking for help with this experience by handing the experience over to the Universe. See the difference?

Surrender and trust go together. Release your attachment to the outcome and trust that everything will work out in the best way. If you have any fear about trusting the Universe to support you, let that go as well. When you trust that everything will work out, it will.

By surrendering you allow in the best possibility and probably one you did not dream of being possible. When you surrender and trust, you stop worrying and it gives you time to get in balance.

Do not let your ego or well thought-out plans keep you from letting things work out in the best way possible. Control is an illusion of the ego. Unfortunately, this illusion limits you to a few choices, if that, when you are actually full of possibilities. Instead, know that you are a creator with the Universe. You are here to have experiences and no matter what, you are always supported.

Magically, things work out the moment you trust in something bigger than a well thought-out plan, especially when that plan is just not working out. The moment you surrender a situation, you create a space for intervention from the Universe. This creates space for a miracle to come in, something you could not have planned or prepared for. Basically, when you surrender, you allow space for an intervention from the Universe.

Often, the hardest part about surrendering is the fear of losing everything. Know that you will not lose something you are supposed to have. Material objects are just that, objects. As you know, objects may make you happy for a small amount of time, but in the end, they mean nothing. You will not take them with you when your body passes. However, you will take your experiences with you. If there is a way to make what is a seemingly difficult time easier, would you like to do it?

The answer is to surrender and trust that everything will work out in the best way possible. The key to this is trust. Trust in something bigger than yourself, something bigger than your ego, and trust that everything works out every time! Trust that the Universe supports you in every moment, because it does. You just have to let the Universe support you and it will.

Surrender and Trust Exercise

If you keep trying to do something and no matter what you do, it is just not working out, surrender it. Let it all go. Then trust that everything will work out perfectly for everyone involved.

White Light: Bring the White Light through the crown of your head, into your feet, and into the Earth. It is a steady stream and you feel safe, comfortable, and at peace.

Letting go: Imagine gathering all of the obstacles, problems, or issues you are having at this moment and letting them go. Release all the frustration from trying to make things work out how you envisioned. Let go of the specific outcome you had in your mind. Imagine it all flowing up into the Universe and disappearing. Let it all go.

Surrendering: Imagine handing this situation over to the Universe and surrendering any fears and control over the "ideal" outcome. As you are sending this up into the Universe, know that the Universe will support you. All is well. Everything will work out in the best way possible for everyone involved.

Receiving: Allow abundance to flow into your chest or heart area from the Universe. Begin by opening your arms up into a wide "V," as wide as you can comfortably stretch your arms. Let the rainbow flow into your chest, and then flow gently around you. You may see the individual colors of the rainbow or an actual rainbow.

Say: "The Universe supports me. I am love. All is well," or you can say whatever feels right to you. Sit like this for a few moments.

Open your eyes when you are ready.

Tips: At this moment you are not asking for anything from the Universe. You trust that everything will work out as it should. If you ask for things or ways you think it should work out, this exercise will not be very effective. You have to surrender control of the situation, your ideal or planned outcome, and trust that it will work out perfectly, and it will. What you believe to be true is what you create.

If you find yourself having a hard time trusting, what letting go should you do? What is preventing you from trusting the Universe? After you do the letting go, fill yourself with your "I am" statements, and try the "Surrendering Exercise," again in a few days.

After you have surrendered, remind yourself if you start to worry or stress about this again, that all is well. You do not have to worry. Trust the Universe and allow the Universe to do what is supposed to be done. The Universe will work things out in the best way possible for everyone involved, you just have to step aside and let it happen. If you find yourself getting stuck, try doing some letting go, regain control of your thoughts, and do something that will help you get back into balance in this moment.

Chapter Reminders

In every moment there are things you control and things you do not. You always control how you respond and how you are using your energy.

If you find yourself trying to control a situation and it just is not working out no matter how you try, stop. Surrender the situation to the Universe. Trust that it will work out in the best way possible. Then, focus on getting back in balance.

Letting go is an active process where you are trying to release thoughts, beliefs, energy, etc., from your being. Surrendering is when you hand a situation over to the Universe and trust that it will all work out perfectly. Surrender and trust go hand in hand. After you surrender a situation it is a perfect time to focus on getting in balance.

Balance will help you be in a better place for whatever is next in your journey. The more in balance you are, the easier you will flow with whatever is happening around you. Balance will also give you something tangible to focus on while you are waiting for things to sort themselves out.

6 – Rebalance

When it feels like nothing is happening during change you may feel stuck and like you are not moving forward. However, when things are stagnant, it is so you can have some downtime to rebalance and prepare for what is next. When you feel stuck, use that time to let go of any frustrations with this change in your life and to nurture yourself too. Take this time to support yourself so that when things feel busy again you are recharged, balanced, and ready to go.

Sometimes, the thought of taking a break seems scary because it gives you more time to think about what you have to do or your fears about this change. However, taking a break helps you get back in balance so you know how to course correct. How do you know what steps to take when you feel overwhelmed and out of balance? Instead, do something to help you rebalance, then come up with your plan.

Downtime often comes before things get busy. By getting in balance when things are slower, you will be in a better place to handle whatever is next. Then when things do get busy again, you will feel ready to go, not overwhelmed. You are not a machine, nor can you function like one. Balance is essential during change!

Often, balance is like a pendulum swinging and it is important to notice when the pendulum is swinging too far from your center. You will also find that by taking the time to get back in balance you have more energy and a renewed purpose. Afterwards, you will be happy you did. In this chapter, learn to nurture yourself and balance your whole being. As you read this section, think about what kind of support would nurture you right now on your journey.

Nurture Yourself

There are many different ways you can give yourself support. Support means many different things depending on what is going on in that moment. This section gives you some ideas on different ways for you to give yourself the support that will help you through stressful, difficult, or tough times.

Create Downtime

Downtime is critical no matter how crazy or stressed out you feel. In your fast-paced, wired, always on-the-go world, life is typically busy. Throw any type of change into that mix and you will notice that you start to feel overwhelmed and you can use some extra support. Planned or spontaneous downtime can be refreshing.

Unplug: Take a break from always being plugged in and aware of what is happening with your family, friends, and work. Unplug from your phone, internet, computer, laptops, tablets, email, social media, and any other technology when you can. You will find this to be very freeing!

Take time to enjoy something you like to do outside in nature, play, spend time with a loved one, or read a book. Instead of feeling rushed, enjoy yourself and whatever activity helps you to unplug. What would help you unplug?

Just "be": Sometimes, you may feel frozen as if you cannot let go or move forward, especially when a lot of events have happened all at once in your life. This is a space to just "be" for a small amount of time so you can process everything that has just happened before you take action.

Take time to "be," whether this is going for a walk, reading a book, watching a movie, being by water, or whatever you feel will support you in this moment. Use White Light, pastel colors, or rainbows to support you during this time.

Do not check out, instead use this time to process and be objective. Let everything sink in before you move forward. Sometimes, you have to let events catch up with you before you know what to do next or what actions will best support you.

When you are ready to start taking action, begin with letting go of any frustration, tension, or beliefs that are no longer supporting you. Then, you can create a plan that will support you and you can start taking action. Take one step of your plan and see how it goes or you may find that surrendering and trusting instead of following a plan will support you more. As always, do whatever supports you the most in this moment.

Re-energize: Pamper your body. Get a massage, go to the spa, get a facial or pedicure, take a nap, go to bed early, go out to eat, or do whatever will help you feel recharged and pampered.

Regardless of what you decide to do during this downtime, the goal is that whatever you do, you will feel better after you did it. Recharge! You are not meant to go-go-go all the time.

Schedule Lightly

Notice how quickly your calendar fills up? One way to become aware of this early on is to put all your plans, events, and meetings onto a calendar that shows you a monthly view. This will allow you to space things out and not overbook yourself.

If you start to notice a week looking too busy or full, rearrange your schedule by moving plans that do not have to happen that week. When your schedule is extremely busy with things that you have to do; make sure you schedule in a carefree day. Put an "x" onto any days or times that week where you can take a break.

Sometimes, you think something has to happen in a certain time, but that does not necessarily mean it has to be done in that time frame. What deadlines are you setting for yourself? Make sure they are realistic and not overwhelming. You do not have to cram everything in. See what can move to another week or even month if you do have a lot of stuff happening.

When your calendar is overwhelmingly busy, it throws you way out of balance. The change in your life is already throwing you curve-balls; make time in your schedule to adjust to these as well. If there is time in your schedule for last minute things that have to be done, you will not feel overwhelmed.

Plan a Carefree Day

Schedule at least one day a week that is not full of a single plan. No schedule, no clock watching at all that day. This is especially helpful when you are going through big or life-altering changes.

In the beginning, you may feel more comfortable scheduling one day each month. Then you may move to a whole weekend once a month, and then try to have one day each week with no plans. Start with what you are comfortable with, even if you can only get in a couple of carefree hours. You will cherish this time and find time to plan more carefree days.

A day that is empty! Imagine looking at your calendar and knowing that you have this day to take a nap, recharge, play, or have fun. An added bonus, you get to flow with the day and not watch the clock. Time will feel like it is moving slower and you will feel free.

Perhaps you make one day a resting day and the next time you have a fun day. Find what works for you and helps you find the most balance. Perhaps you schedule a fun day and when the day appears, you decide you would rather have a day of rest. Do what works for you; always check in with yourself.

You already have so much going on in your life, schedule this carefree day on your calendar right now. Make it happen! What day can you schedule for yourself this month? If you cannot commit to a whole day at first, when can you schedule in a couple of carefree hours this week?

Go With the Flow

Sometimes, the most carefully laid plans fall apart because something else comes up. In that moment, you have a choice. Do you try to desperately cling to what you originally were going to do and find that it really did not work out that well? Or do you go with the flow of the day instead?

Going with the flow is often very rewarding and feels

miraculous because you did not plan it; you flowed with a plan that formed for you instead. When you are going with the flow, it means that you are not holding onto any expectations or events that you had planned, especially when it starts falling apart. As things shift and change, you flow and shift with them. If an appointment or meeting gets cancelled this gives you time to do something else that was on your list for the day or it makes room for something else to happen. Perhaps, if you are feeling overwhelmed, this cancellation gives you an opportunity to recharge.

Going with the flow does not mean that you are ungrounded or feeling as if you are floating like a kite. Rather, it means that you adjust your day based on what is going on around you and how you are feeling.

Try going with the flow on a busy day. Notice how you feel and how much better the day flows. You will find that it is possible to go with the flow quite often and things work out better when you do.

Celebrate

Take time to celebrate your successes and the work you have done thus far. If you just keep going and going, you will burn out. Instead, create time to relax, be pampered, or have fun.

Celebration is an important piece to balance. It helps signal the end of something big and makes way for a new beginning. Celebration also helps you appreciate your experiences and the work you have just done.

Depending on what you have been experiencing will determine the best way to celebrate your successes. Sometimes, the most pampering thing is a hot shower or bath, comfortable clothes, and downtime. Other times, you may feel an urge to dress up and do something special. Check in with yourself and see what feels like the best celebration and do it.

Find a balance with celebration. It is important not to do it too much or not often enough. If you feel like celebrating something, that is a sign you should do it. Sometimes, it is important to celebrate the small steps with small celebrations if you are working towards something big. Other times, you may decide to wait until you accomplish your goal. Always do what works best for you and do it in a balanced way for you.

Balance Your Whole Being

You probably favor one part of your being, whether it is your body, mind, or spirit, (connection to the Universe). Most people favor their mind or their spirit. The part of your being that you favor is the part that you give the most attention to. What part of your being do you give the most attention? Why do you favor this part of your being? Who or what experiences helped shape this for you?

Body

Often the body is ignored and not considered a key element. However, the body tells you just as many things as your spirit and mind. Your body will tell you things such as: when it does not like something, when you are pushing it too far to do things, where you are storing your energy, and what would support you in a moment. Think about how your body tries to give you messages or clues. Do you listen or brush them aside until you are forced to pay attention?

Mind

If you only focus on your mind, you are ignoring your body and spirit. Your body and spirit may be trying to give you clues that things are not working. If you are focusing on your mind, your mind will rationalize away these clues until something happens that stops you and forces you to listen. Does this sound familiar to you?

Spirit

The spirit is able to guide you; it is your internal navigation. Often, it shows you parts of the puzzle and what steps to take next but the spirit does not experience time slower like the body and mind do. You will find that your intuition moves quickly. Sometimes, you may think things will happen sooner than they actually do. The spirit is energy and moves faster than the physical manifestations around us. Make sure that what you are doing is in balance with your body and mind.

Roles of Your Being

One part of you is not better than any other part of you. Every part of your being has a purpose, which is why there are multiple parts to your being. The more you focus on balancing your whole being instead of one part of your being, the easier things will be. This is also how you create balance in your life.

Each part of your being works together but individually they have roles:

Body: Acts as a sensor and is the physical part of your being. Helps you get around, lets you know what is supporting you or hurting you, and helps you become aware of where you store energy in your body.

Mind: Rational and more rigid than the other two parts of your being. Your mind helps you by sorting, organizing, and making sense of the information around you.

Spirit: Helps you instinctually and is energy-based. This part of you knows something that may not be explainable, is an internal compass you can always trust, and is the energy in which we all connect to each other.

What strengths do you have to add to these parts of your being?

Make sure you are focusing on all of your being and notice the information each part gives you. If you value all of your being, you will notice that it all flows together. Each part has a role and together it creates a whole. However, if you continue to focus on only one part, that part will seem dominant and you will be missing out on some valuable information and balance.

Check in and notice if you have any letting go to do about why one part of your being is more valuable than another. Consciously be aware of all the parts of your being, their roles, and their messages to you. Make an effort to check in with all of your being throughout the day until it becomes natural to check in. Pay attention to the clues it gives you. You will find that they work together to help you if you listen to all of your being's messages.

Chapter Reminders

In every moment, you can get back in balance. Sometimes, you can do something simple like connecting with the White Light, a pastel color, or a rainbow. In other situations, you may have to plan something to do later, like letting go or planning an activity that will pamper you. Focus on knowing that you are going to do it and see if there is anything you can quickly do in this moment to help you now. You are always supported in every experience. Trust the Universe to take care of the details.

Changing your busy and over-planned routine is sometimes the best support for you, especially on weekends or days you can be more carefree with your time. If you find every minute of your day has been planned and you are overwhelmed when last minute things happen, stop the craziness. Days like that are too much and push you over the edge easily. Balance is essential! Look at your schedule and see where you can schedule in time to nurture yourself and balance your whole being.

You will notice that being in balance is more like a pendulum swinging, not a stagnant state. The goal is to keep the pendulum from swinging out too far one way or the other. Getting in balance does not have to take a long time, it can happen in seconds. Getting out of balance can happen just as quickly. Make sure that you check in with yourself so that you are nurturing and supporting your whole being.

It is easier to take care of yourself before something happens that forces you to take care of yourself. What are some ways you can nurture and connect with yourself? How do you know when you are out of balance? What are some things you can do to get back in balance?

7 – Energy Awareness

The more positive you feel in any moment, the more empowered you will feel. The more empowered you feel, the more life flows. Why? Because you aren't getting stuck on any of the "junk" - negative thoughts, criticism, judgment, etc., that holds you back from your potential. What you give with your energy is what you receive.

Being aware of what you are doing with your energy will help you course correct much faster than if you are subconsciously going through the motions of life. Instead of just doing what you always do, stop and look objectively at why you are doing something. Then check in and see if it is still supporting and helping you. If it is not, it is time to do something new.

Take time to reflect and become aware of what you are doing with your energy, especially when you feel like things are not working out. Instead of getting frustrated because things are not working out, find out what caused this shift in the first place and course adjust. During big and life-altering changes it is important to be aware of what you are focusing on, to understand how your life patterns are shaping your experiences, and the best way for you to get help and work with healers.

Your Focus

Your mind is in overdrive when you are stressed. Your mind is good at categorizing but sometimes the categorizing goes a little crazy if you are not paying attention to what you are focusing on. How much time and energy are you spending on running different scenarios through your mind on either things that already happened or on things that are yet to come? How much time do you spend trying to control events in your life? Has this helped you feel calmer or did it make you worry even more than you already were? Remember, whatever you focus on you attract to yourself. Worry attracts more worry just as peace attracts peace.

In each moment, you begin anew. You were upset, worried, or scattered a minute ago, great. That was your experience in that moment. That is over; it is now a new moment. Moments and energy shift that quickly. What would you like to create in this moment? What steps will you take to create this reality? What exercises in this book will support you? You can look at the "Exercise Contents" to help you find the exercise that will support you right now.

Shifting your focus is that simple. The more aware you become of where you are putting your energy, the easier it is to shift your focus off of things that are not supporting you. Then it gets uncomfortable for you to be in a place where you feel chaos. Why feel chaos when you can be in a place of peace?

Enjoy your Experiences

The day flows by very quickly when you are not aware of where you are focusing your energy. The more you put your energy in the past by judging how you could have done things differently takes away from this moment. As does worrying about what is going to happen next or in the future. If you find yourself completely checking out, you will feel like a bystander with time passing by quickly. How can you focus on this moment instead?

Throughout the day, check in with yourself and notice what you are focusing your energy on. The more you focus on enjoying and living in this moment, the more time you will find you have in the day. By living in the moment, the day will go by slower. How often do you feel like the day has gone by slowly instead of quickly?

Take a mental picture of the moments that you truly enjoy. If you start taking more mental pictures, you will not feel like life is rushing by you. Instead, you will remember the things you did in that moment instead of everything being a blur and not remembering many details. Part of your journey is to enjoy your experiences and to remember those moments.

Enjoying the Moment Exercise

Take mental pictures of special moments to help you remember and treasure them. You will find that this helps slow time down and helps you enjoy the moment.

White Light: Bring the White Light through the crown of your head, into your feet, and into the Earth. It is a steady stream and you feel safe, comfortable, and at peace.

Appreciate: Enjoy what is happening around you in this moment. Feel the energy of this moment through your whole being.

Take a mental picture: Appreciate what is happening, as it is happening, and literally imagine taking a picture of that moment in your mind. You are taking a picture of how you feel and what is happening. You will not only remember that event but you will remember feeling good about it.

Tips: Do not focus on anything that hurt you, instead focus on the experiences that brought you joy, love, and peace. Make sure you are feeling that positive energy run through your being, and into the Earth. If you start to feel ungrounded, bring the White Light through your being again.

White Light: When you are finished, bring White Light through your body and into the Earth to help you balance your being.

Open your eyes when you are ready.

Stop Judging Yourself

Who has the right to judge you?

You will probably say that you do, but really, no one does. Not even you.

No one has right to judge you because they do not know everything that you are experiencing or the purpose of your experience. Just as you are not able to see the whole puzzle at one time, no one else can see that for you either. How do you know what you are judging when you can only see small pieces of the puzzle at a time?

Judging takes a lot of energy. Energy that you can be using for something that will help you instead of hurt you. If you find yourself judging yourself or someone else, freeze the thought. Remember, you are only seeing a small piece of the puzzle. You do not know all the details, therefore, you cannot judge the situation. Let it go and instead, be grateful for something in that moment.

Life-altering changes take quite a bit of time so they often lead to a lot of self-judgment. Remember to surrender your irritations, frustrations, and anything preventing you from enjoying this moment. Trust that everything will work out because it always does. Think about other experiences where you have trusted and it worked out. You can also say the mantra, "Everything always works out in the best way possible for everyone involved."

Surrendering, trusting the Universe, and getting in balance will help you through this change, not judging yourself. When you look back at this period of time, you will appreciate all these visualizations and exercises that helped you through this experience. You will remember parts of this change being hard, but you will focus on what helped you get through it. You will get through it. You always do. Instead of judging yourself, focus on doing what will nurture and support you.

Your Life Pattern

You have routines you follow throughout the day. Weekday routines are different than your weekend routines. Typically your most important routines are your morning routine and your bedtime routine. In a way, your routines are like a ritual. They prepare you for something and often you just go through the motions of doing them without thinking twice about it.

Life patterns are similar to routines. Life patterns are something that you do over and over again subconsciously in certain situations without even being aware of what you are doing. Often, they can become a routine, in the sense that when you are faced with a certain trigger, you react in the same way without even thinking. Sometimes, the life patterns are familial, meaning you feel something has to happen a certain way because that is simply what happens in your family and it happens to everyone in your family. Therefore, the familial life patterns must happen to you too.

These life patterns are ways that you are using your energy and creating your life without being aware of what you are doing. Often, they are extremely emotional as you are pulling in a lot of fears and triggers from this life and other life experiences. Typically the triggers are fear-based. Often, you are reacting with a deep-rooted, emotional response that may not even make sense in your current situation.

Triggers vary for each person, but some examples are: fear of not having anything, fear of getting hurt emotionally or physically, fear of being abandoned, etc. If something happens that is a trigger for you, what do you do? What is your pattern? Is it a familial pattern? Where do you feel this life pattern in your body? How does it affect your energy? Is this fear valid in your life right now? What can you do to let go of this fear?

These life patterns create your reality. Sometimes, they make you feel powerless or hopeless, as if life is "just this way." The question then becomes, how else can your life be? If you think, "No one supports me." You are right, no one will. The same thing happens if your life pattern uses phrases such as: "I do not have enough." "Nothing works out for me." "I have to be ready to run at any moment." "This happens to everyone in my family." What phrase do you use? Whatever your life pattern is saying, you are creating. This often leads to a downward spiral where in the past you did not know what to do. Now erase all those phrases as these are not something for you to create.

Since you are becoming more aware of your life patterns, you can change them and course correct if they are not supporting you anymore. You have continued to have this life pattern because you believed it to be true. Now that you are aware of it, you can heal it and let it go. Once you let it go, you may find it trying to reappear into your life once in a while. If it does, you will know what is happening and be able to stop it right away and shift your focus.

When you find yourself reacting to a situation and your first response is getting really emotional; stop, breathe, and check in with yourself. What is really going on? What is the fear? Is it valid in this situation? If not, let it go by doing the "Anchors to Ashes Exercise."

Anchors to Ashes Exercise

Let go of the anchors and life patterns that are no longer supporting you. Then fill that space with colors, rainbows, and "I am" statements that support you.

White Light: Bring the White Light through the crown of your head, into your feet, and into the Earth. It is a steady stream and you feel safe, comfortable, and at peace.

Awareness: Become aware of where you store this life pattern in your body. Where are the anchors? Check in with yourself and find them. Anchors are typically in two places; they are connected together and energetically plug in where they are anchored.

Tips: When you bring the White Light through your body, notice where you feel tension or heaviness. This is where they are. Then notice where an energetic line runs through your body that connects them together.

If you are dealing with a familial life pattern, notice where you are connected to it through your family. Your family will be the anchor. When you surrender this tie, you are not surrendering your connections to them, just your connection to the life pattern.

Surrender: Release any fears in your body from the anchors and the line. Let them all go. Give them to the Universe. You can do them both at the same time or individually; do what works for you.

White ashes: Go to where one of the anchors is plugged into you, whichever one you are drawn to the most. Begin by beaming White Light into that area. As the White Light travels the energetic line, it turns the energetic line of that life pattern into white ashes. Imagine the ashes blowing away and disappearing into the White Light. Continue to do this until both anchors and the line are gone.

Colors: Imagine filling your body with a soft color that is comforting to you. Whatever color pops into your mind first is what you should use.

Then imagine your body having hundreds of tiny specs of that supportive and nurturing color all over your body. Imagine the specks growing and touching each other. They fill every part of your being. Your body surrenders to that color, releasing anything that is left to release. You feel calm and at peace.

Rainbow: Bring a rainbow in from the crown of your head, through your body, into your feet, and into the Earth. Stay in this place for a moment and feel the rainbow flow through your body.

"I am": Then fill your being with: "I am love. I am light. I am safe. I am whole. I am free." Then you can add another "I am"

statement or mantra to support the area(s) where you just released the anchors if you would like.

White Light: Bring White Light through your body and into the Earth to help you balance your being.

Open your eyes when you are ready.

Next time you start to experience the trigger- pause, notice the trigger, and then let it go. Do the "Anchors to Ashes Exercise" again if you feel the anchors coming back and prevent yourself from recreating this life pattern. Simply let it go, let the power it had over you disappear. Say, "I am safe. I am whole. I am free."

Working with Healers

Healers are becoming main stream in our society again. A shift is quickly happening in our world and many healers are being born to heal the things it is time to heal. People are feeling a pull to work with healers to help them heal things in their lives that they do not know how to fix.

Healers are Born

There are a lot of genuine healers out there and just as many people who believe they are healers. Everyone has access to certifications and labels, but having a certification or label alone does not make one a healer. Of course, healers probably do have some labels and certifications because our society expects healers to have them. Just remember that healers are born, they are not made. You will know when you are in the presence of a healer. They lift your energy in a way that others typically cannot just by being around them.

Healers have many abilities and they are able to move energy in ways that are unique, effective, and healing for themselves and other people. Abilities are a guiding compass that help people know what to do and when. Everyone has abilities to help them heal in their own life. Some people use their abilities how they are supposed to, and sometimes they do not use them at all.

Healers have been healing across most, if not all of their life experiences. They intuitively know what to do and how to help you based upon what you are experiencing. Healers do not focus on a small piece of you; rather, they always focus on healing the whole being.

Trust your Instincts

If you do not feel comfortable working with someone, then you should not work with them, absolutely no questions asked. You know who you should and should not work with. You will connect with someone and know they can help you or you will feel a pull to run in the other direction.

Follow your instincts and it will make things easier for you. These feelings are often based on other experiences with this person in other lives. There is more on this in the next chapter. However, if you do not feel safe, please know that this is not the person to help you with your energy or healing. Always work with people you feel a connection with and that make you feel safe. Otherwise, you will have an experience, but probably not a healing one at that time.

Learn from healers but do not become dependent on anyone else to know what to do. Remember, you have abilities and they are your internal compass. Use your abilities to help and guide you. If you get stuck and do not know what to do, connect with a healer to teach you how to get back on track. Remember, the tools you use now may require tweaking to help you in the future as you change and grow.

At all times, it is important for you to check in with yourself and make sure the work you are doing is supporting your whole being. If you feel like something is not working, it is not. What else can you do instead? You should feel better after you have worked with a healer. If you do not, then try something else instead.

Chapter Reminders
Pay attention to where you are putting your energy and what you are focusing on. Whatever you focus your energy on, that is

what you create in your life. Make sure that you are creating experiences that you would like to have and that support you. Your power is in this moment. What are you focusing on?

Your life patterns are complex and important in your journey, especially when you change them. You probably have not paid much attention to them; they have simply become routines. Life patterns are things that you do subconsciously every time you interact with your trigger and often you feel out of control while it is happening. Notice when you start living your life pattern and change that life pattern if it is not supporting you anymore. Familial life patterns are patterns you take on because you believe you should. If they are not working for you, release them.

Always know that you have the power to fix yourself. You put energy and experiences in your body throughout the day and you have the ability to remove that energy. You can let healers help you and teach you, but always be aware of what you are intuitively getting to do to heal yourself. Be aware of the power you give yourself and the power you give to others.

8 – Everything is Connected

Everything is connected like a spider web. Nothing is alone or separate. Everything has a purpose and is part of something bigger. Life is about having an experience that makes you feel like an individual but at the same time you are literally connected to everyone else. You can feel this connection when you bring the White Light through your being. In that moment, you do not feel separate. You know that you are a part of something bigger. You are me, and I am you.

You choose to have the experiences in your life to heal parts of you from this and other experiences. Every experience is an opportunity to return to love and light, and to remember that negativity and darkness are not real. In every moment you can choose love or the absence of love. Love is always possible because anything not of love is an illusion and it disappears in the light.

While you may not understand why things happen the moment they happen, you will understand at the perfect time. Nothing happens randomly. There is always a reason, a way for you to heal, and an opportunity to return to love. You are always supported no matter what is happening around you. Your actions not only affect you, but those around you as well.

Use this chapter to help you understand some of the other

pieces in motion in your life, especially during big and life-altering changes. Absolutely everything in your life has a purpose and at all times you can return to your true state, a being of love. Everything in life is woven together. Just like the spider web, what you do to one part of the web, affects the whole web. You experience this in your life with karma and how energy is reflected.

Understanding Karma

Karma – what you do to others you do to yourself, instantly. The moment you are mad at someone else you feel it instantly. Just as the moment you are happy with someone, you feel happiness instantly. Karma is not a bad thing. Simply, it is a way to feel what you give to others.

Karma also happens across lives as a way to heal any experiences that were not of love and to help you return to being whole. Remember, you are a being of love and your natural state is to be whole. Some of your experiences happen so that you see the areas in your being where you are fragmented. Once you are aware, you can release whatever is there and become whole again.

You have every experience in your life to experience it, learn from it, and then return to your true state of being, love and light. Your mind categorizes your experiences, and as it does, it labels them as good or bad often based upon what is acceptable in society at that time. What this means is that your experiences are not good or bad. They simply are. Every experience has a purpose and happens for a reason.

Karma and Other Life Experiences

Past lives or other life experiences have a direct impact on the karma you are experiencing in this life. In essence, you are living and experiencing all of your lives at once. This means you are able to experience karma from those other experiences now because those experiences are happening now. This is a very difficult concept for the linear mind to understand, but you have access to all your lives right now. Your other lives are tangled in this life experience so you can become whole in any experiences that left you fragmented.

Connections Across Lives

Sometimes, you will experience an intense connection to a person or an animal that you do not know in this life. For example, you may feel pulled to someone you do not know and feel that you have an intense connection with them. On the flip side, you may meet someone and you feel a pull to run in the other direction. Perhaps you are drawn to an animal and because of this connection you adopt it. In all of these scenarios karma is appearing so something can be healed for you, something can be healed for the other person or animal, or for both of you.

Objectively Heal Other Experiences

Karma is also at work when you experience something intense emotionally and it makes no sense with your current life. This is an experience that is ready to be healed now. For example, if you were abandoned in this or another life, there will be things happening to help you let go of anything you are still holding onto from that experience. Perhaps you do not trust anyone and you think you have to do everything yourself. You probably do have support now, but you do not use it because you are afraid of being abandoned again. If you are experiencing anything like this scenario, you will learn how to heal that experience by doing the next exercise, "Healing Across Lives Exercise." Any intense emotions that you are feeling now that do not make sense in your current situation often are karmic experiences that you can objectively begin to heal in this moment.

The more objective you are, the easier it is to heal an experience. You experience karma in multiple lives to heal something with someone that you may not be able to heal in one life. Perhaps in this experience, you are less attached to what is happening in the other life. That makes it easier to heal part of or all of that experience in this life, which means that you heal it equally in that life as well.

You may find that there is a lot of healing to do and it is not all from this life. Sometimes, you may find that there are layers to be healed, just like when you are doing a letting go session. Some healing will happen in this life, some is to be healed in other lives.

An Energetic Shift

At no time are you being punished. When you do heal something in this life, it has an immediate effect on all your other experiences. You will feel a shift now and in that experience as well. This is another difficult concept for the mind and ego to grasp because it is not linear and concrete. Instead of questioning why you feel an energetic shift or how it is possible, appreciate that you healed a past hurt. These karmic experiences help you release the energetic fragments you are carrying in your being so you can become whole again.

Notice when you are doing your letting go session and other experiences appear in that session, how do you feel when you let them go? You feel free instantly. Also, at some level you know that it makes an impact across your existence in that moment, you can feel the shift. You instantly feel lighter and happier in multiple lives.

Healing Across Lives Exercise
Let go of any emotional tie to a past experience that is affecting this moment. The experience(s) can be from childhood, your past in this

life, or from another life experience. Then, fill that space with love.

White Light: Bring the White Light through the crown of your head, into your feet, and into the Earth. It is a steady stream and you feel safe, comfortable, and at peace.

Letting go: What past experiences or emotions are you holding onto that are literally preventing you from moving forward in your life? Where are they at in your body? Let them go. Surrender them to the Universe.

Appreciation: Appreciate this experience for happening in your life. Everything happens for a reason; perhaps this happened so you could release it. What did you learn from this experience? How has this experience shaped you? How are you stronger because of this?

White Light: Bring the White Light through your body.

Pastel colors: Fill the space in your body where you were holding onto this experience with a soft color that is comforting to you. Whatever color pops into your mind first is what you should use.

Rainbow: Bring a rainbow in from the crown of your head, through your body, into your feet, and into the Earth. Stay in this place for a moment and feel the rainbow flow through your being and align your energy.

"I am": Then fill your being with: "I am love. I am light. I am safe. I am whole. I am free." Then you can use another "I am" statement or mantra that specifically replaces the experience you just released.

White Light: Bring White Light through your body to help you balance your being.

Open your eyes when you are ready.

Karma Reminders
Karma Happens Instantly

The Universe is here to support you and remind you that you are love. Karma happens instantly, it does not torture you repeatedly until the end of time. Instantly means that the moment you do something, you feel it in this life and in other experiences. The moment you heal the energy in your being from that experience, you feel it now and across other lives as well.

If you hurt someone else, know that you feel the pain immediately when the act is done. Often, you will feel this across many, if not all of your life experiences with that person. Everything is connected, so this act is experienced everywhere immediately so that it can be healed. When you heal that experience by returning to a place of love and light, you will also feel it across your lives.

The next time you get angry or frustrated, try approaching these situations from a place of love. You will be amazed at how quickly things shift. An added bonus is that you will not do something you will be sorry for later. Energy moves quickly especially when love is involved. Love is your truth and it conquers all.

Karma is not Punishment

You may feel that karma keeps happening over and over again to punish you. Remember, karma happens instantly and across lives. Karma is instantly feeling what you have done to someone else. The moment you heal that energy fragment in your being, you no longer feel that karmic experience in other lives.

On the other hand, life patterns are patterns you create for yourself over and over again. This happens because you believe this pattern to be true so you keep doing them until they no longer support you. If you do not like a pattern in your life, change it!

The only punishment that is happening in your life is any judging, negative talk, self-doubting, or criticism that you are doing to yourself. You are the one who punishes yourself, and it is not necessary. If you surrender the situation and let go of anything you are holding onto, you will free yourself. Do not judge your experiences from the past or as they are happening. Instead, look for what part of you is fragmented and is ready to be whole. Then heal it.

Energy is Reflected

Like attracts like in your life which means that what you are putting out, you will receive from those around you. Fear attracts more fearful experiences. Anger attracts more anger. Love attracts love, just as peace attracts peace into your life and surroundings. If you do not like what is going on around you, take a look at your energy and what you are giving off into the Universe. What you give off energetically in a moment is exactly the energy you will receive.

Relationships operate in the same principle of like attracts like. Sometimes, a person will have an experience so they can act as a mirror for you. This means that whatever is happening in their life is also happening to you, but you can see it more clearly in their situation. Perhaps a friend is limiting them self or a family member is stuck in a self-destructive pattern. Often someone is helping you by acting as a mirror for you. Maybe you are doing the same thing they are doing and you are not aware of it. Ask if this is happening in your life in some way and what you can do to change it.

Karma is also reflected as a mirror. You are able to see exactly what you are doing to someone else. This means that we act as a mirror for each other since we are each other. If you get mad at someone and you say something to hurt them, that person is a mirror for you. This action is literally reflected off of them and back onto you instantly. You will be the person that walks away sad, angry, or mad. Why? Since we are all one and connected, you hurt yourself. It is not possible to hurt someone else without immediately feeling the result of that hurt. Literally, what you do to others, you do to yourself. Karma acts as a mirror.

Peace begins with you just as anger begins with you. You affect those around you and what you give off, you receive. You appear to be separate from me because of your ego. The ego is there so that you can have this experience of feeling separate, even though you are not. By remembering that your life is a mirror and that your actions are being reflected back to you helps you see things more objectively. Once you realize this is happening, you can begin to heal experiences. You can also spread more love, light, and peace and it will be reflected back to you.

Love is all there is. Worry, stress, fears, and concerns are all illusions. You know this to be true because they disappear in the ball of light. The ball of light reminds you that we are all one, we are all connected, and that we are all beings of love. Nothing else exists in this ball because if it is not of love, it is not real and it simply disappears.

Ball of Light Exercise

We are all connected. You are supported in every moment, and only love is real. If you do not see it in the ball of light, let it go!

White Light: Bring the White Light through the crown of your head, into your feet, and into the Earth. It is a steady stream and you feel safe, comfortable, and at peace.

Visualization: Imagine the White Light in a ball shape. It is light and airy. Know that you are a part of this ball of light. You are surrounded by love. Love radiates from the ball.

Surrender: Let go of any tension, frustration, or worries. Surrender them to the Universe and watch them disappear into the White Light. Notice how you feel in the ball of light. Keep surrendering anything that is not of love until you have no worries at all. Feel the peace, support, and love flow through and around you.

Tips: In the ball of light, love is all there is. Notice that everything in the ball radiates love to you, through you, and around you. Nothing else is real. If you find yourself floating in the ball, bring the White Light through your being and then rejoin the ball of light.

You may also see gold sparkles in the ball, a gold color, or another color that supports you at this time.

Mantra: Say and know, "All is well. All is as it should be."

Open your eyes when you are ready.

Chapter Reminders

Everything is connected because we are all one. Nothing happens to punish you or hurt you, rather every experience is an opportunity to heal and return to love. Love is light. White Light fixes everything the moment you return to it. Anything not of love is not real, it is an illusion and it disappears in the light, always.

Karma happens instantly and you feel it instantly and across applicable lives. Karma happens as a way to heal experiences that were not of love and to help you return to being whole and full of light. Life patterns will happen repeatedly in your life until they no longer support you. Do not confuse them with karma.

Like attracts like. What you put out into the Universe comes back to you. You are able to see this in your life like a mirror. Imagine that what you are doing in the mirror is what you are creating in your life. If you are in a place of love, love bounces off the mirror and back to you.

If you are unhappy with how things are going in your life, check in and see what bigger thing is happening. Why is this happening in your life? What can you do to return to a place of love and balance? What part of you is ready to be healed? Then do the exercises that will help you.

9 – Enhance Your Practices

Experiences happen constantly that shift your energy and your mood. If you are aware of what is happening and how you are responding, you can get back into balance quickly. Once you start experiencing balance more often, you will find that you purposely choose balance over chaos. There will be no place for long term chaos or things that are not supporting you.

The key is living consciously; being aware of what you are doing and why you are doing it. Make sure that you are checking in with yourself and that what you are doing is nurturing, supportive, and in alignment with your purpose. Otherwise, why are you engaging in it?

Empower yourself as much as you can on your journey. Surround yourself with people that nurture and support you. When you are in a stressful period of time or going through many changes, check in with yourself more often and course correct as necessary. Transform your practices if they are no longer serving you by engaging in practices that do. Throughout this book you have been learning about energy exercises that can transform your life when you practice them. Enhance your practices by truly practicing your rituals and spread love in your actions.

Truly Practice Your Rituals

As a society, spirituality typically focuses on spiritual practices and rituals. Spirituality and religion are often intermixed as if they are one and the same, and they can be. Often times, it boils down to if people are truly practicing what they preach or are they just going through the motions.

Sometimes, people absentmindedly go through a spiritual ritual they were taught, and the intention and purpose behind the ritual is gone. Sometimes, it just becomes something to do, not something that helps you or others in any way. Do you have any rituals like this?

In our society, more time is spent just showing up and going through the motions because if you show up, that is what counts, right? Unfortunately, energy does not respond to that. The energy is not there if you do not fully participate and are not fully present in what you are practicing. Physically being there, but being energetically checked out does not support you or anyone. What you give energetically is what you get energetically; it is mirrored back to you.

Make sure that whatever spiritual practices you engage in, you are truly doing at an energetic level. If you find that you are not engaged energetically or that the practice is no longer supporting you, perhaps it is time to find something that will engage and support you. You may also find that if you are going through a big or life-altering change that adding more practices and support will be very helpful to you at this time. Some ways you can truly practice your rituals are by trusting your intuition, enhancing your rituals when they are no longer supporting you, and by praying in a new way.

Trust Your Intuition

Trust your intuition or instinct; it is your internal compass and navigation. Your intuition is a part of you that simply knows things that the mind cannot understand or explain. Whether your instinct is guiding you away from danger, course correcting you on your path, or guiding you towards a miracle, it is your guiding light.

Your intuition is a way that you are able to connect with the Universe. The way that you experience intuition can be the same every time or it can vary, especially if you are not listening to it. Your intuition will come to you in different ways to get your attention if you are ignoring it. Sometimes, you will hear something, other times you will see or feel something, and sometimes you just simply know.

There is no good or bad way to connect with and be guided by your intuition. Just pay attention to it. If you are hearing, seeing, or sensing something, there is a reason for it; pay attention. Do not ignore it. If you do not know what to do with what you are receiving, ask the Universe what you should do with it, and you will know.

Know that what you get intuitively is not set in stone, rather it is fluid. Free will happens and things shift. This does not mean you are not connected with your intuition, it just means that things change. Let your intuition guide you when this happens.

Do not continually test your intuition. When you first start paying attention to it, you may test it to see if it works or if it was a random event. However, once you know how to recognize your intuition, any testing is wasting your energy. Instead of trusting and going with the flow, you may find yourself playing a constant game with the Universe of, "When and how will this happen in my life?"

As you can imagine, playing games and testing the Universe serves no one, especially if you are experiencing a big or life-altering change. The moment you start playing, the Universe will find other ways to help you and get your attention, and things can get confusing. Perhaps things around you will start falling apart or not working out how they typically would. If you notice this happening, ask yourself what you should be doing and how can you course correct. Then do it. Use your intuition as a tool to help guide you through this change in your life. Your intuition can help you in ways other people or things cannot.

Enhance Your Rituals

Participate actively in spiritual practices that elevate you and that make a difference in you and those around you. Otherwise, you might as well do something else that will support you more than going through a ritual in an absent-minded way.

If you find yourself struggling to stay present during a practice or ritual it may be time to do something else that will support you. If someone told you to do something five years ago, chances are it should be tweaked. You are not the same person you were a year ago, much less five years ago. As the energy of the collective whole shifts, you shift and as you shift, your rituals should too. Are there any spiritual practices or rituals that you are doing that are not supporting you anymore? What else can you do instead?

Many people practice their spiritual rituals because someone told them to do something in a specific way. They do it without questioning what they are doing or achieving. Whatever you are practicing, you should feel better when you are done. You should feel uplifted, centered, grounded, and balanced.

No matter who is telling you to do something with your energy, it is important that you check in with yourself intuitively to make sure that it is what you should be doing in that moment. If you do not trust or agree with what they are advising you to do, chances are it is not going to work for you. What works in one situation does not always work for every situation. Just as what helps one person may require a tweak or two to help someone else.

Instead of idolizing any spiritual teachers, follow their examples. Idolizing prevents you from doing the spiritual work they are teaching you to do. It allows you to focus on glorifying their work, but not necessarily practicing it in the world. You will feel stuck or trapped if you idolize them. If you practice what they do, you will feel empowered because you are doing the work.

Life is about course correcting and this includes shifting when your spiritual practices are no longer supporting or working for you. Often, the changes in your life are helping you course correct these spiritual practices too. Make sure whatever you are doing supports you and those around you as well.

A New Way to Pray

Whenever anything big happens during change that is beyond your control, chances are you will pray. Even if you do not usually pray, there are situations in life where you will find yourself praying. In your prayer you will ask for what you would "ideally" like to be the end result.

Typically, instead of trusting the Universe to solve whatever the problem is, in prayer you ask for it to be resolved in a specific way. The hiccup with this approach to praying is that you are only able to see a small piece of what is happening, not the whole puzzle. How do you know what to ask for? How do you know what is the best thing? If this prayer is for someone else, how do you know what will help them the most?

Instead of falling into this pattern the next time something big happens, trust the Universe to solve it by praying in a new way. Remember, this is where miracles happen. Surrender the situation to the Universe, trust that everything will work out in the best way possible, when and how it should. Then send White Light. Typically when big things happen, they throw you out of balance with stress and worry. Instead, send White Light as a prayer and then do something to get back in balance.

Sending White Light as a Prayer Exercise

Surrender a situation that affects you or someone else to the Universe so it can be resolved in the best way possible for everyone involved.

White Light: Bring the White Light through the crown of your head, into your feet, and into the Earth. It is a steady stream and you feel safe, comfortable, and at peace.

Visualization: Let go of any fears, concerns, or worries you have about this situation. Release them to the Universe. Imagine them turning into a speck of light as it travels up into the sky.

White Light: Then surround the situation in White Light. Know that the situation is filled in love and surrounded by love.

Surrender: Surrender this situation to the Universe. Release any attachment you have to the situation and the outcome.

Trust: Trust that everything will work out as it should. Remember if you start to worry, you will be sending worry to yourself and that situation. You can also focus your mind on a mantra like: "All is well. All is as is should be. Everything always works out in the best way possible for everyone involved."

White Light: Bring the White Light through your being again and let it flow into the Earth.

Open your eyes when you are ready. Check to see if you are in balance. If you are not, take this time to do something to help you get back in balance.

Spread Love in Your Actions

Every thought you think, every word you say, and every action you make impacts you and those around you. We are all connected, so the more you share love, the more we flow in love together. From this place, we are able to connect and transform our world into one of love and peace, our natural state of being.

You cannot always control what is happening around you, but you do control how you respond to it every single time. How you respond affects those around you. If you spread love and happiness, it is returned to you. Spread love wherever you go. Smile at others in the store, smile at the cars next to you in traffic, and smile at the people you see when you walk into a building and mean it! You will find it is contagious and it will show you that like really does attract like. In every situation, ask yourself how you can show love.

What you give out is returned to you instantly. When you feel love, peace, calm, and gratefulness, feel it through your whole being. Let it radiate out to those around you and notice it being returned to you in that moment. If you find yourself in a place where you are out of balance and grumpy, course correct immediately. Find a tool in the book to help you, even if you just randomly open up the book to any page; that page will be perfect for you in that moment.

Love is transformational. You can experience this during your change(s) by experiencing peace and knowing that all is well. The moment you return to a place of love, you transform whatever experience you are having into one of love as well. This helps us all.

Peace is a Choice

Peace is possible in every moment. Peace is a choice. At first if may seem like it is the harder choice and that sometimes it is easier to be angry, mad, or frustrated. However, you will find that peace is easier and takes less energy than conflict, stress, and turmoil.

Conflict is hard on everyone involved and it takes a lot of energy to be in that place. The more we fight, the unhappier we are. Just think about the karma at work in conflict! Being in any type of conflict takes more energy because it is not your natural state.

Peace on the other hand is something that everyone can experience even in times of chaos or loss. You may have some letting go or surrendering to do at first. Then you will find that peace is there and you are a part of it. In every situation, love is there. Let it shine through you and into your surroundings.

Gold Sparkle Exercise

This exercise reminds you that peace is possible in every moment. No matter what you are experiencing, love conquers all.

White Light: Bring the White Light through the crown of your head, into your feet, and into the Earth. It is a steady stream and you feel safe, comfortable, and at peace.

Let go: Let go of any tension, frustration, or irritation in your body. Release anything you are trying to control; surrender the situation to the Universe.

Visualization: Imagine your body is filled with small, gold sparkles. They are warm and comforting.

Imagine the sparkles growing slowly and spreading their warmth, as they turn into a warm light filling your being. The light radiates from the inside of your body to your surroundings. Say, "I am love. I am light. I am safe. I am whole. All is well. "

Trust: Know that you are love, supported, nurtured, and peace. Imagine the gold sparkles flowing into the environment around you, sharing this energy. Know that all is connected, all is well, and all is love. Know that the Universe supports you and everything around you.

Tips: Feel free to use other colors instead of the gold if that is what you are getting to do. You may even do a rainbow of colors. Do what works best for you in this moment.

White Light: Bring the White Light through your crown, into your being, and into the Earth.

Open your eyes when you are ready.

All is Well

Life does not have to be complicated, even during big and life-altering changes. Most movies, television shows, and books tell you otherwise, but drama does not have to be a part of your life. Simple is in! You just have to choose simple over complicated.

Take things one step at a time. This not only makes life easier but it makes it more enjoyable. During life-altering changes, it can be very difficult to plan more than one step at a time because so many things are shifting and uncertain. In this place, fears are able to creep in easily and grow quickly until you return to a place of light and love. Sometimes, when you do not know what to do, the best action is to trust that all is well. Then it will be!

"All is well," is a powerful mantra. Simply saying this mantra will help you feel better about whatever is happening in your life and create a sense of peace in your being. Your energy is guided to a place of trust instead of worrying about what is happening now or next. If all is well, there is nothing to worry about. Instead, you can enjoy the peace this mantra brings to you.

All is Well Exercise

Use this exercise to help you surrender your next steps in a situation to the Universe when you do not know what to do.

White Light: Bring the White Light through the crown of your head, into your feet, and into the Earth. It is a steady stream and you feel safe, comfortable, and at peace.

Let go: Let go of any fears surrounding this situation. Let them flow up into the Universe and disappear.

Mantra: Say, "All is well." Feel the energy of these words flow through your being from your crown, into your feet, and into the Earth.

Tips: If the fears come back, remind yourself that all is well and feel the positive energy from those words flow through your body. If they keep coming back, you may have more letting go to do.

White Light: Bring the White Light through your crown, into your being, and into the Earth.

Open your eyes when you are ready.

Chapter Reminders

Make sure that you are always doing what feels right and what will support you in that moment. If you are only going to go through the motions, save your energy until you are ready to consciously participate. What you put into your practices is what you will get back out of them.

Know the purpose of the practices you are doing and make sure they are supporting you. Check in and see if there is a way to make them more effective or if something else should be done instead. As you grow and change in life, you will find that what worked in the past may not work anymore. This is okay. Try other rituals and practices and see what will support you.

Peace truly is possible in every moment, even in times of loss or chaos. Truly, it is easier to be in a place of peace than not. Peace is a natural state that we can return to in any moment.

"All is well." Use this mantra to help your focus shift from one of fear and worry to one of trusting the Universe. Everything always works out as it should and because of this, all is well.

***

Energy Balance

This is your guide to not just getting through change, but to transforming your life into one of balance. Surrender and trust go hand in hand. When you surrender, you are trusting that everything will work out perfectly, and it will. Surrendering and trusting are more passive activities which give you time to focus on balancing your being. The more in balance you are, the easier it will be for you to flow through the changes in your life. Enjoy your experiences and if you find you are not able to do that, what exercise will support you in this moment?

You are here to have experiences and heal past hurts, but remember to have fun too. Life is a journey of many experiences, enjoy the ride. Have as much fun as possible and remember that balance is possible in every moment. Balance your energy from within.

About the Author

Lisa is the author of "In Light & Love: My Guide to Balance," and "Energy Awareness: My Guide to Balanced Relationships." She has been working as an Intuitive Energy Coach since 2002 and writes these books to help her clients and others get back into balance. Lisa was born with her intuitive abilities with energy healing and is a Reiki Master.

She has the ability to see, sense, hear, and feel energy. Lisa intuitively knows why, where, and how each person stores energy within their body, how to release that energy, and how to reprogram that area with positive energy.

Lisa currently lives in San Diego, California with her family. For more information about Lisa, her videos, and her events, visit www.lisagornall.com.

Follow her on Facebook at facebook.com/lisamgornall, Twitter @LisaMGornall, and on Instagram at energycoachlisa.

Made in the
USA
Columbia, SC